AAMIR KHAN

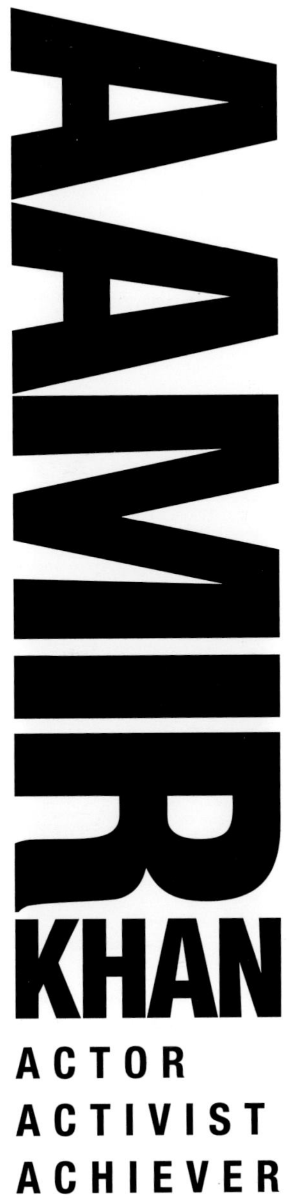

PRADEEP CHANDRA

NIYOGI
BOOKS

Overseas Distribution

USA and Canada
ACC Distribution
email: sales@accdistribution.com
www.accdistribution.com

United Kingdom, Ireland, Europe and Africa
Kodansha Europe Ltd
email: info@kodansha.eu
www.kodansha.eu

Cambodia, Burma, Laos and Thailand
Paragon Asia Co. Ltd
email: info@paragonasia.com
www.paragonasia.com

Published by
NIYOGI BOOKS
D-78, Okhla Industrial Area, Phase-I
New Delhi-110 020, India
Tel: 91-11-26816301, 49327000
Fax: 91-11-26810483, 26813830
Email: niyogibooks@gmail.com
Website: www.niyogibooksindia.com

Editor: Shaurya Shaukat Sircar
Design: Write Media

ISBN: 978-93-83098-29-3
Year of Publication: 2014

Printed at: Niyogi Offset Pvt. Ltd., New Delhi, India

Dedicated to
Dr Mukesh Batra

CONTENTS

Aamir Khan relaxing at his home in Bandra; behind him is a painting gifted by Salman Khan.

FOREWORD

by Rajat Sharma

Aamir Khan: An Obsession

I met Aamir Khan for the first time on the sets of *Aap Ki Adalat*, the television show I hosted. It was the summer of 1998. His film *Ghulam* had just been released. He arrived in his *tapori* (vagabond) look with a tight-fitting vest, leather jacket and biker gloves. During the show, on the audience's demand, he sang '*Aati kya khandala*', the song that became a rage in the country. And then he stunned everyone present in the studio by narrating how he almost died performing a stunt for this film. He jumped in front of a running train to make the scene look realistic. Aamir got saved by a fraction of a second from being run over by the train. Such is his obsession with his work.

When Pradeep Chandra told me that he was doing a coffee-table book on Aamir Khan, I thought it would be a challenge. Aamir has so many colours in his life that it would be almost impossible to compile all of them between the covers of a single book. At the same time, I had trust in Pradeep's ability. I have known Pradeep for over thirty years. I have great memories of working with him. When I was the editor of *Onlooker*, he was my favourite photographer.

In early 1980s when we did a cover story on Amitabh Bachchan, Pradeep produced not only some outstanding pictures but also gathered a lot of interesting stories from the life of the superstar. A couple of years later I was working on a cover story on Dhirubhai Ambani and Nusli Wadia. It was the most bitterly fought war between two tycoons. There were hardly any good pictures available and these two never allowed any photographer to go near them. The night I completed the cover story, Pradeep was in the office with me till midnight, but we had no pictures to finalise the cover. I was booked on a flight to London the next morning. Pradeep told me, 'Sir, don't worry, please go, I will get the pictures.' True to his word, he did come up with wonderful pictures of Dhirubhai and Wadia.

In June 1985, I did a cover story on Chandraswami. It was the first sting operation where Chandraswami was completely exposed as being a conman. Chandraswami was obviously raging mad. I got to know that he was in Mumbai meeting celebrities. I was tempted to do a follow-up story and needed photos for it. But my reporters and camera persons were not allowed anywhere near him. Pradeep once again came to my rescue. He not only managed to get photos of Chandraswami but also captured in his camera, film stars Raj Babbar and Smita Patil paying a visit to the controversial god-man. Pictures showed that Raj and Smita were carrying tiffin for Chandraswami.

I am aware that Pradeep loves challenges. He is obsessed with his camera and his pictures are his life. That's why his pictures are unusual. Each of his photographs tells a real-life story.

I am also aware that Aamir is hardly bothered about stories or pictures of himself. He perhaps is the only one who declined the offer to pose for his wax statue at Madame Tussaud's. Who else but Aamir would have the guts to stop doing commercials and lose nearly 100 crores while running a crusade against the oft hidden, inherent ills in our society with *Satyamev Jayate*, his first reality show for television. This is what makes Aamir different from other film stars. He is undoubtedly one of the most successful actors, but he never behaves like a superstar. He is passionate about using his creative skills to give a message to people. However, he does not want to use his stardom to enter politics or become a full-time activist. Aamir is brilliant in his thinking and his personality is unique.

I still remember the anecdote he had mentioned about the making of *Lagaan*. He narrated how Javed Akhtar told him that his idea of making such a film was suicidal. Aamir had actually approached Javed to write lyrics for the film. After seeing the script, Javed told him that it is a sure-shot recipe of a flop film. Aamir replied, 'Javed Sahib, I am going to make it because my heart says so. If you don't want to write for it, it's ok. I won't feel bad.' Javed said, 'When you have decided to commit hara-kiri, let me also contribute.' *Lagaan* turned out to be a super hit. But this was not just about *Lagaan*. Every time Aamir said yes to a new film, someone close to him would tell him this would be a disaster. When Aamir started work on *Rang De Basanti*, his sister warned him. She told him that already four films had been made on Bhagat Singh and one more on this subject would be a dud. Aamir ignored the advice. *Rang De Basanti* went on to become a huge success.

When Aamir shared the subject of *Taare Zameen Par* with his friends, each one of them told him that it sounded like a documentary on dyslexia. They told him, 'This time you are bound to sink.' The film was a real victory for Aamir and his beliefs.

Aamir is a success story because he believes in himself. He thinks from his heart yet works from his head. While working on a project, he gets completely lost in his work and disconnects from the world. After he did *Ghajini* where the character loses his memory every fifteen minutes, Aamir told me that for many days he actually used to forget faces and incidents. During an episode of *Aap Ki Adalat* in 2013, he narrated that after playing Bhuvan in *Lagaan*, for many days he used to stand with his entire body weight on both his legs, head up, chest out, just like Bhuvan did in the film.

Aamir amazed me when in *3 Idiots* he played a college-going guy at the age of forty-four. He used to have a controlled diet, spent hours in the gym and conditioned his mind to feel like a teenager. I was very surprised that he lost weight without losing the glow on his face. His energy levels were high. I asked him the secret. Aamir took me to his diet specialist Dr Vinod A. Dhurandhar in Mumbai. What the doctor advised after few tests was quite complicated. He drastically cut down my calorie intake and yet wanted me to eat every two hours, a healthy diet of eggs, biscuits, fruits, carbohydrates and vegetables. It was too complex for me. Aamir took me to his house, sat down on the floor and in minutes drew out a detailed meal plan. I will never forget his concern and personal touch. Of course, the diet plan worked for me, and I lost ten kilos in four months. I still owe it to Aamir.

My faith in my friends has always kept me going and I am sure that readers will find Pradeep's book on Aamir Khan different from the usual coffee-table books.

The writer is Editor-in-Chief, India TV

AUTHOR'S NOTE

s I sit to pen down my thoughts on Aamir Khan, the 'thinking' actor, I realise that in a way I have an old connection with him and was destined to write this book.

Decades ago while I was still studying, I had met Raj Khosla who was then making *Do Raaste* and was having some problem with his still photographer. He looked at the pictures of Rajesh Khanna I had shot and asked me if I could do the stills for his film. He gave me his Rolleiflex 120mm camera with a 2.8f lens and asked me to report for the shoot next week at Mehboob Studios where Rajesh Khanna and Mumtaz were going to do a song sequence, '*Chhup gaye saare nazaare oye kya baat ho gayee*'.

Later his nephew, Bolu Khosla realised I did not have the set-up to make the prints. The Khoslas made a darkroom for me in Raj*ji*'s garage which happened to be in Marina Apartments—the same building where Aamir lived since childhood. While doing my research I found out that Raj*ji*'s daughter Reena Khosla was a close friend of Aamir as a kid. Raj*ji* would often call me home for drinks and end up playing the harmonium and singing K.L. Saigal's songs. Once he asked me, 'Can you write?', and showed me a book on women's attire. He said that I must travel round the country shooting pictures of different traditional dresses worn by women, make notes and then write a book. That must have been the first instance when someone suggested that I author a book and today as I write about one of the legendary actors in the Indian film industry, I cannot forget Raj*ji*'s prophecy. It is a beautiful coincidence to write a book on his daughter's best childhood friend Aamir Khan. In a way this book is also my tribute to my first employer Raj Khosla with whom I worked in *Do Raaste* and partly in *Mera Gaon Mera Desh*.

In spite of the fact that I started my career in films and my first published picture was of actor Waheeda Rahman, I must clarify that I am neither a film journalist nor a film photographer. I have always worked with newspapers and magazines like

The Indian Express, *The Times of India* group, *The Free Press Journal*, *The Independent*, *The Illustrated Weekly of India*, *The Week* and several others.

I clicked Aamir for the first time at the launch of his debut movie, *Qayamat Se Qayamat Tak* (*QSQT*) and most recently at the music launch of *Dhoom: 3* at YRF Studios. Over the years, there have been a few interactions and many opportunities to shoot him for the various publications I have worked with.

When I was with *The Indian Express*, my colleagues at *Screen* told me that Dev Anand was shooting at the Cricket Club of India (CCI) for *Awwal Number*. I rushed to the venue and that is where Dev sahab introduced me to Aamir. Dev sahab had known me for decades and I shared a warm relation with him. I shot a lot of pictures of Aamir and Dev Anand which later got published in *The Indian Express*.

In earlier days, since the press were not restricted on film shootings, photographers and journalists were welcomed there. During those days I had clicked Aamir on the sets of several movies like *Love Love Love*, *Dil*, *Deewana Mujh Sa Nahin*, *Daulat Ki Jung*, *Aatank Hi Aatank*, *Dil Hai Ke Manta Nahin* and *Baazi*. The producers and directors would then happily pose with the actors for photo shoots. The trends have changed now and today films are shot in secrecy to guard an actor's look for the movie until the film is ready for release and the media gets invited for promotional events.

Once I went to Juhu beach in the wee hours of morning to cover a cycling race and was surprised to find Aamir there. He was fiddling with his cycle and preparing himself to take part in a cycle race from Juhu to Otters Club, Bandra in order to promote his upcoming film *Jo Jeeta Wohi Sikandar*. The photo feature appeared in G magazine edited by Bhawana Somaaya. Unfortunately most of these images are not with me, but a few from the series that I could dig out have found a place in the book.

When I was working with *The Illustrated Weekly of India* edited by Pritish Nandy in January 1991, we were discussing as to who should be on the next cover. We wanted someone from the film fraternity as we had already done lots of political cover stories. Nandy said, 'Aamir Khan, COOL', which later became the headline of the story. Sandeep Bamzai, a sports reporter had just joined us from *The Indian Express* and was assigned to do the story. Sandeep asked, 'Sir *main* [me]? I am a sports reporter' to which Nandy replied, 'Don't be a frog in the well. You can do this! You will have a different perspective since you are not a film writer'. That was another instance when I met Aamir Khan.

On one occasion while Rauf Ahmed was editing *Filmfare* and I was with *The Weekly*, he asked me if I could shoot some pictures of Tahir Hussain and Aamir together. I had known Rauf since the time I first came to Mumbai to join a film magazine *Super* that Rauf had brought out and later shifted to launch the magazine *Movie* for the IBH group. He would often give me some freelance assignments to shoot. Rauf was one of the few editors who had a great visual sense and hence I always enjoyed shooting for him.

I went to meet Tahir Hussain who asked me to be comfortable in his home and while we were chatting, Aamir entered neatly dressed with his shirt tucked into his trousers, well combed, looking fresh and smiling. He reminded me of Dev Anand. We shot some pictures, more of mood shots rather than making it glamorous. We chose a few spots like inside his house, in the surroundings and near his car. Just then a young girl walked up to him and wanted to be clicked with him. Since Aamir agreed, I did a couple of shots with her too. It was a very satisfying shoot.

During the shooting of *Ghulam*, the PR person Rajendra Rao invited me to shoot some images of the song '*Aati Kya Khandala*' being filmed at Fantasy Land, Andheri (East). I spent the whole night there taking photographs of the song sequence, which got published on the cover page of *Bombay Times*. In fact, I even lent a transparency of one of the pictures that appeared on the film's poster.

I met Aamir on a few occasions while working with *DNA* and found him to be a very warm-hearted person. We did a photo shoot with him and Imran Khan for the front page of *DNA* at Nasir Hussain's bungalow. There was another shoot we did at Famous Studios for a Mumbai story with him sitting on the steps having a cutting *chai* (tea) and *vada pav* (a spicy potato burger) as he read a book. I asked him to look into the camera and he said, 'That would look most unnatural with me reading a book and gazing into the camera at the same time!' I must mention how much he loves to gorge on *vada pav* and while going for the shoot I had picked the same for him along with a small glass for having tea. During another shoot at his Khar office, I bumped into him in the elevator and he was happily munching away on a sandwich. My editor Ayaz Memon had asked me to get a *Ghajini* poster autographed by him. The picture also appeared on the front page of *DNA*.

Aamir has always been cooperative with the photographers. To celebrate the 25th anniversary of *Qayamat Se Qayamat Tak*, he held a press conference at Film City and even cut a small cake. Aamir invited one of the photographers, Pradeep Bandekar, to come up and cut the cake with him as he had been seeing him for several years on all important occasions capturing his images. This gesture showed the actor's sensitive side.

It's been a long and wonderful journey while writing this book and learning about the man behind the actor and his iconic status.

INTRODUCTION

Papa kehte hain bada naam karega,
Beta hamara aisa kaam karega
Magar yeh toh koi na jaane
Ki meri manzil hai kahaan...

Nothing else can really sum up the brand called Aamir Khan—the Indian matinee idol who is still chartering his life's trajectory in multiple reel and real roles. He is not just a superstar. He is a super actor or to be more precise, he's a combination of both. He can change from being a militant (in *Fanaa*) to a college student (in *3 Idiots*) to an art teacher (in *Taare Zameen Par*) and yet he makes each role his own. You zoom out from Aamir the star and zoom in on the character he portrays. Aamir is perhaps the only actor from the Hindi film industry who has a 100 per cent track record at the box-office in this last decade or so. You may call him a maverick; you may call him a marketing genius, but the fact remains that brand Aamir Khan spells success. He is an astute producer and director as well. Like Sun Tzu, Aamir is a master of the tactics in *The Art of War* and knows how to wait and watch before pouncing on the opportunity and annihilating all opposition.

Dadasaheb Phalke (1870–1944), the pioneer of the Indian film industry.

In the evolution of Indian cinema through the last 100 years, in every quarter of a century, a single individual has become the mighty force that swayed the course of the film industry—whether it was the pioneering efforts of the filmmaker Dadasaheb Phalke or the screen persona of the Dilip-Raj-Dev trio or the phenomenal ascent of superstars like Rajesh Khanna and Amitabh Bachchan.

Each individual contributed to the development of film history and introduced a new era. In the latest quarter of the Indian cinema's century, Aamir Khan has driven it towards a new dimension combining these talents and adding his own unique stamp. The first quarter saw the rise of singer-actors. The next had talented actors ruling the roost as actors and producers. The one following that saw the rise of superstars with exclusive fan clubs. Actors were no longer just performers and producers. They are now constantly exploring new mediums to remain in the public eye. Stars endorse FMCG products, appear on television and also do stage shows abroad.

In his twenty-five-year movie career starting from his earliest days as a teenybopper heart-throb in *Qayamat Se Qayamat Tak* (*QSQT*) till now, Aamir Khan has the ability to ruthlessly reinvent himself across many different mediums. Aamir Khan is today a mega-horsepower entity as the industry makes another paradigm shift in its interface to keep audiences glued globally. He is the most formidable Khan who has made his presence felt as an actor, producer, director, crusader on television and is also the face of *Incredible India*. He is above the perception of appreciation in the form of awards. He gets ample rewards via a large fan following as a superstar. His marketing strategies to promote his films have hit the bull's eye each time.

We trace the journey of how this brave and spirited soul of Tinseltown became an icon for a cross section of generations. He is quintessentially a 'Bandra boy' from cosmopolitan Mumbai. Aamir Khan commands admiration for his honesty and integrity in whatever he does. As a child, he was deeply influenced by his cinematic lineage. He also has a distant and quiet connection with Indian polity from the days of the Independence struggle. He is a descendant of freedom fighter Maulana Abul Kalam Azad. Growing up in Pali Hill, Bandra West (India's equivalent of Beverly Hills), he honed his talent as a tennis player at the Maharashtra state level.

Above: Amitabh Bachchan.

Facing page: Aamir at the launch of the first song of Dhoom: 3.

At the age of eight, Aamir made his debut as a child artiste in Nasir Hussain's Yaadon Ki Baaraat.

However, the love for cinema proved to be more overpowering. As a child of eight years, he made his debut in the famous producer Nasir Hussain's film *Yaadon Ki Baaraat* (1973), who was also his uncle. He assisted his uncle on the film sets of *Manzil Manzil* and *Zabardast* and did a short role in friend Ketan Mehta's *Holi* in 1984 before his debut. He preferred to learn the nitty-gritties and all possible nuances of filmmaking before undertaking the voyage of being one of the most accomplished and sought after actors of Hindi cinema. He won a billion hearts with his debut in *Qayamat Se Qayamat Tak* (1988), which is now considered a classic in the annals of film history. Aamir's chocolate boy looks could have become a tool to his survival in films. But a string of few flops made him circumvent and reinvent his strategy to remain a successful hero. Sometimes called the 'Tom Hanks of India', Aamir has worked in all genres of films successfully. His forthcoming attractions generate enough interest for audiences worldwide to make a trip to the nearest movie theatre.

The 'thinking man's Mr Bollywood' continues to make a strong impact ever since he started off in the Hindi film industry. He knows his brand name carries weight and is responsible enough to do things that accentuate his stature today. His early years were very influential, as they have shaped his very nature. Some women in his life have altered his pursuits of perfection. Yet they remain private. He derives his strength from the thinking of these women who have impacted his public behaviour. Little wonder then the opening episode of his mega-crusade on television dealt with the issue of female foeticide. He acknowledges the contributions of the various women in his life—both public and private.

With his debut in Qayamat Se Qayamat Tak *(*QSQT*) with Juhi Chawla, Aamir won a billion hearts.*

As an actor, Aamir has dabbled in different genres and proved his versatility with his risk-taking ability. He has managed to be pitch-perfect in the last decade. Be it period films like *Mangal Pandey* and *Lagaan*, or contemporary flicks like *Dil Chahta Hai* and *Ghajini*, or the *tapori* (vagabond/rowdy) roles he played in *Rangeela* and *Ghulam*—he has been convincing and versatile in his portrayals. He has successfully tackled sensitive subjects like dyslexia (in *Taare Zameen Par*) and the current education system (in *3 Idiots*) that later became one of the highest grossers in the history of Indian films. As a producer, he actively backed new filmmakers with a good script like *Peepli (Live)* who needed a platform to tell their story. Very few superstars in the past have supported the efforts of another filmmaker in this manner. In another twist to his career as a producer, Aamir introduced a new genre of film like *Delhi Belly*. His foray into television with *Satyamev Jayate* has been appreciated for the sensitive way in which he handled hard-hitting subjects.

His movie *Lagaan* in 2001 was nominated from India for the Oscars in the 'Best Foreign Language Film' category. At the 2010 Melbourne Film Festival during the screening of his film *Peepli (Live)*, Aamir was introduced as the 'Johnny Depp of Bollywood'. He stated, 'The Hindi film industry should emerge as the best in the world, and that's what I aim to do whenever quality cinema is mentioned'. Aamir has even spoken about Indian films in universities abroad.

His earlier films that did not run successfully taught him some hard lessons of life that everything is not acceptable at the box-office. He mastered the art of rebuilding himself. He works by his own rules and keeps setting new ones in the business. He now chooses winners almost all the time. Aamir started working on a single film at one time when other heroes were doing multiple shifts. He set the rule of accepting only bound scripts. His healthy and fresh looks prompted other heroes to go to the gym for six- and eight-pack abs. He also started the trend of refusing awards! Now there are many other actors who are doing the same, but the credit goes to Aamir for this path-breaking decision. Even after so many years, he still sticks to his stand of not accepting awards.

Adopting the classic 'method' approach to acting, his reasoning, questioning and logic have often irked his co-stars. He has brought forth the issue of giving importance to the real heroes of a film—the writers. He has stated boldly, 'I desire to open a school for writers where they have full freedom to express

Aamir addressing the audience at the 'Innovation for India Awards 2008'.

their creativity and imagination. Suppression and exploitation of writers only leads to half-hearted work and eventually a bad movie with no soul, which is my concern'.

Aamir Khan is acknowledged today not only as an impressive actor and dependable producer, but also as an influential public figure. He wields his inspirational disposition beyond the world of cinema. As a believable star, he brings value addition to his brand by promoting causes and issues that affect people. After a lot of consideration and deliberation, he associated himself with the Narmada Bachao Andolan by supporting Medha Patkar. He studied the situation and problem carefully before lending his name and support to the team. He received flak for his behaviour and his upcoming film *Fanaa* was banned in Gujarat. Even senior actress and activist Shabana Azmi did not spare her attack on him. When his effigies were being burnt, not one person from the industry raised any alarm. But, Prime Minister Dr Manmohan Singh came to his rescue and support. Aamir has been silently supporting the Jan Lokpal bill initiated by Anna Hazare. Unlike other superstars that have remained silent on burning topics that inflict our country, Aamir has shown the courage to move

with conviction. He is not the one to do a mere 'entertainment show for charity' for a cause and then disappear. He actively involves himself and leads the way. All the humanitarian causes he supports have been genuine efforts as a useful public figure.

In 2013, Aamir Khan featured on the cover of Time *magazine as one of the 100 most influential people in the world.*

Facing page: During a song shoot for Ghulam *at midnight.*

In May 2013, Aamir Khan featured in *Time* magazine's annual list of the 100 most influential people in the world. The list, now in its 10th year, recognises the activism, innovation and achievement of such individuals. The Managing Editor, Richard Stengel of *Time* says, 'The *Time* 100 is not a list of the most powerful people in the world, it's not a list of the smartest people in the world, but it's a list of the most influential people in the world. They're scientists, thinkers, philosophers, leaders, icons, artistes and visionaries. They are people who are using their ideas, visions and actions to transform the world and have an effect on a multitude of people.' His name features alongside the who's who of the world, including politicians like US President Barack Obama and famous Hollywood actors. At the *Time* gala held at Lincoln Centre, New York, on April 23, several Hollywood actors were present. Among them was three-time Academy Award-winning actor Daniel Day-Lewis, who won it recently for the lead role in Steven Spielberg's 2012 film *Lincoln*.

There is always curiosity about a celebrity's personal life and it is no different with Aamir. His privacy has been subject to the gossip mills time and again. Being a man with the Midas touch, he has had his fair share of ups and downs with the media but he has always moved on without looking back. Aamir thrives in this mad world admirably and it is his self-belief that carries him through— with or without friends. With two marriages and three kids, he has never been apologetic about his marital status. It is private and does not merit public debate. His first marriage to Reena Dutta was his best kept secret, before he made his debut as a hero. He has always remained stoic in the face of controversies—whether it was for the custody of his younger brother Faisal, a tiff with his late father Tahir Hussain or his parting ways with some

A shot from the song 'Aal izz well' *in* 3 Idiots.

close co-stars. Till date, he has not 'poured his heart out' to any journalist on personal issues.

Aamir has closely guarded his public persona revealing bit by bit only when needed. He is a perfect marketing guru, a rare occurrence in Hindi cinema in the last few years. He seems to have developed a carefully carved niche as a role model. It is not only his fans that admire his tenacity as a rugged performer but he has gained the respect of his contemporaries, the new stars on the block and a few rivals. The method actor has managed to get his point across clearly when he refers to a rival's work or more often ignores it. Many things do get swept under the red carpet, but his childlike smile covers any trending dispute that might harm his carefully sculpted image. Aamir reacts to those who attack him on the public platform, but he has never put his foot in his mouth. Aamir Khan is secretive to the extent of keeping a tight lid on a few personal and public matters.

A painting by Samir Mondal depicting Aamir's Ghajini *look.*

But no one can deny that Aamir is a visionary and his brand is still evolving unknowingly like the famous lines of the song from the film *3 Idiots*:

Murgi kya jaane ande ka kya hoga,
Arre life milegi ya tave pe fry hoga...
Koi na jaane apna future kya hoga...,

Honth ghuma, seeti bajaa
Seeti bajaa ke bol
Bhaiyaa aal izz well ... all izz well.

Aamir Khan may be called by his screen names like Raj and Bhuvan or by nicknames like 'Mr Perfectionist', 'Cool Customer' or even 'the golden kid', but he is no novice when it comes to his own life. Is he as reclusive as he is made out to be? Is he a serious person or fun to be with? Why do his childhood influences still show up? Has he grown up or is he still a kid at heart? We have tried and unearthed some secrets of this bankable Khan in the following pages. It is a tribute to this versatile actor, producer, director, icon, part-time activist and brand ambassador—all rolled into one awesome package. He moves on a path less travelled by, both virtually and in reality. This book is an attempt to present a *yaadon ki baaraat* of the most lovable superstar of our times.

PALI HILL

THE BEVERLY HILLS OF MUMBAI

'Resilience. Warmth. It has a very harsh exterior, very soft interior.'

Mumbai in Aamir's words

Dilip Kumar, Raj Kapoor and Dev Anand

Facing page: Aamir at a promotional event for Rang De Basanti.

Mumbai is the cinema capital of India, a city where several memorable films have been made since the time Dadasaheb Phalke, the father of modern cinema, appeared at the forefront. Today, Indian cinema is 100 years old. From time to time, strugglers have come to this city to turn their dreams of becoming actors, producers, musicians and writers into reality. Back then known as Bombay, it had numerous pockets or areas where stars built cozy bungalows with high walls to enjoy some privacy. Eventually, these fanciful mansions turned into landmarks for strangers, fans and locals to navigate their way round those areas. One of the first localities to be colonised by the superstars at that point was Pali Hill in Bandra West. Along the shores of the Arabian Sea in the west, many stars built their iconic homes.

The vicinity provided discretion to their stardom. Large and spacious bungalows dotted hilly locales round Mount Mary

The entrance to the bungalow where Dilip Kumar and wife Saira Banu live.

Basilica, Union Park and Carter Road, right up to the stretch of Khar, Pali Naka. Dilip Kumar was the first star to have a huge home down a leafy lane in this area in 1953. Other stars who followed his footsteps were Dev Anand, Madhubala, Rajendra Kumar and Sunil Dutt. In later years, Reena Roy, Pran and Vinod Mehra too made this area their residence. Today Bandra, queen of the suburbs, is the abode to India's three superstar Khans. Recently, Aamir Khan on his show *Satyamev Jayate* said, '*Yeh Bandra jaisa ilaka surakshit mana jaata hai. Main aapko yaad dila doon ki Bandra woh jagah hai jahan teenon "Khan" rehte hain, ek Dilwala hai (Shahrukh Khan), ek Rangeela hai (Aamir Khan), aur ek Bodyguard hai (Salman Khan)*' [Bandra is considered a safe and secure suburb. I must remind you that the three 'Khans' of our industry reside here. One is the 'Dilwala', one is the 'Rangeela' and one is the 'Bodyguard']. All these celebrities live near each other and yet enjoy total seclusion in their luxury retreats.

It was only in 1954 when Mehboob Khan made the famous Mehboob Studios on the other side of the hill that another landmark was born. When Aamir's father and uncle came to this city they too decided to make their abode in Bandra. Close to Dilip Kumar's house is Nasir Hussain's quaint bungalow built in 1962 which has now been in existence for fifty years. It has been an active hub inhabited by its prominent residents since the two brothers Nasir Hussain and Tahir Hussain came to Bombay to make a name in Hindi films. In 2012, Nasir Hussain's grandson and actor Imran Khan renovated the iconic bungalow and moved into it. Aamir Khan celebrated his son Azad's first birthday at this same place along with his entire family. Aamir still lives in the same housing complex.

The large-hearted and jovial Salman Khan.

Left: Dilip Kumar was one of the first actors to choose Pali Hill as his residence.

Tahir Hussain and Raj Khosla (the noted producer-director) lived in the same building in the neighbourhood. Being an observant child, Aamir had different cinematic influences having lived in

this locality. Inhabited by writers like Gulzar and Anand Bakshi, stars, producers and musicians like Pyarelal, the location already has earned the label of being the 'Beverly Hills of Mumbai'. Close to the sea, the boulevard boasts of the late Rajesh Khanna's house 'Aashirwaad', another well-known landmark located on Carter Road. The road has been renamed Naushad Ali Marg after the death of legendary music director Naushad who lived in the same vicinity. Other eminent personalities who stayed at Carter Road include the 'tragedy queen' Meena Kumari, 'Jubilee star' Rajendra Kumar and actress Leena Chandavarkar before her marriage to Kishore Kumar.

You must be wondering what makes living in Pali Hill so magical for movie stars? It lends an aura of exclusivity along with its affluence. Stars started shifting to this neighbourhood in the early 1950s so that they could live away from the noise and crowds. In highly fortified mansions they were able to enjoy privacy with their families. Film stars do not mind crowds at theatres where people throng to see their films. But when it comes to anonymity and peace, they want to live in secluded locations. During her spinster days the actress Neetu Singh too lived in Pali Hill and even after her marriage to co-star Rishi Kapoor, she continues to reside there. They now live in a huge bungalow called 'Krishna Raj' named after Rishi Kapoor's mother, where son and actor Ranbir Kapoor also stays with them. The actor-sisters Karisma and Kareena Kapoor also have their residences in the surrounding sea-facing apartments. Other popular film personalities

Aamir at ITC Grand Central, Parel, Mumbai.

Relaxing at Mumbai's Sun-n-Sand Hotel.

who live near Mehboob Studios are diva Rekha, the 'King of Bollywood' Shahrukh Khan, veteran actress Waheeda Rehman, 'Big Boss' Salman Khan, actor Jackie Shroff and producer-director Subhash Ghai.

The locality sees fresh faces from the film industry coming to settle here in the hope of getting a slice of stardom and solitude. Aamir's quest to move up and invest in the same suburb that saw the rise and fall of his family's fortunes is a testimony that stardom brings its share of burdens and fame with it. The actor will always remain a famous resident of this beautiful suburban neighbourhood. Whether the place is enriched by his presence or he has been lucky to be a part of this area of Bollywood's real estate is debatable. Most film families are superstitious about their choice of certain locations, places and numbers. For instance, several people in films consider Anand Recording Studio as their lucky charm. It is perhaps the same with Aamir. But there is much more to this superstar than just being the typical 'Bandra boy'. He has risen to greater heights and this is just the start of the evolution of his brand. He has already begun building his own legacy.

The upbeat and effervescent Shahrukh Khan.

Above: The evergreen star, Dev Anand, was Aamir's screen idol.

Today Aamir's home 'Bella Vista' at Pali Hill, Bandra is a notable feature. However in earlier years, Dilip Kumar's bungalow was cited as the benchmark to give directions to any place. His residence was considered as a heritage property of the bygone era of Bandra until it got demolished in 2009. Along with his wife Saira Bano, he continues to be a loyal Bandra inhabitant on the same street in Naseem Bano's dwelling.

Aamir was born in Holy Family Hospital located on Hill Road. He started his schooling from Avabai Petit School and later joined St. Anne's School. After his marriage, he continues to live and work in the same locality. The final sound mixing of two of his highest grossing films *Taare Zameen Par* and *Ghajini* have been done at Anand Recording Studios, which is a stone's throw away from his house. It belongs to his screen idol Dev Anand with whom he worked in *Awwal Number* and whose penthouse has been reconstructed into a high-rise. Aamir has always admired Dev sahab for his suave style and discipline. The area is populated by a healthy mix of people of all religions. In a sense, the 'Bandra boy' is a product of the cosmopolitan society that has been the home to progressive families of Catholics, Parsis, Muslims and Hindus—all living in harmony.

genealogy

'My name is Mohammed Aamir Hussain Khan'

An individual's personality, to a great extent, is shaped by his life experiences and the influences of near and dear ones. These influences can be inspirational or otherwise. It is also the bloodline that adds to the charisma of a person. In the case of Aamir Khan, his ancestry has traces of two distinct worlds—politics and cinema. His impressive political lineage leads to Maulana Abul Kalam Azad, a freedom fighter during the British rule. The other is the creative heritage, which runs actively in the family through his father Tahir Hussain and his uncle Nasir Hussain. The current Khan brood consists of his favourite cousin Mansoor Khan and his sister Nuzhat, along with Aamir's own brother Faisal and sisters Nikhat and Farhat. Aamir is the second child and first son born to producer Tahir Hussain and his wife Zeenat. Though very little is known about Aamir's connection with Maulana Abul Kalam Azad, he is very proud of his association with him. The fact that the actor and his wife Kiran Rao have named their son Azad Rao

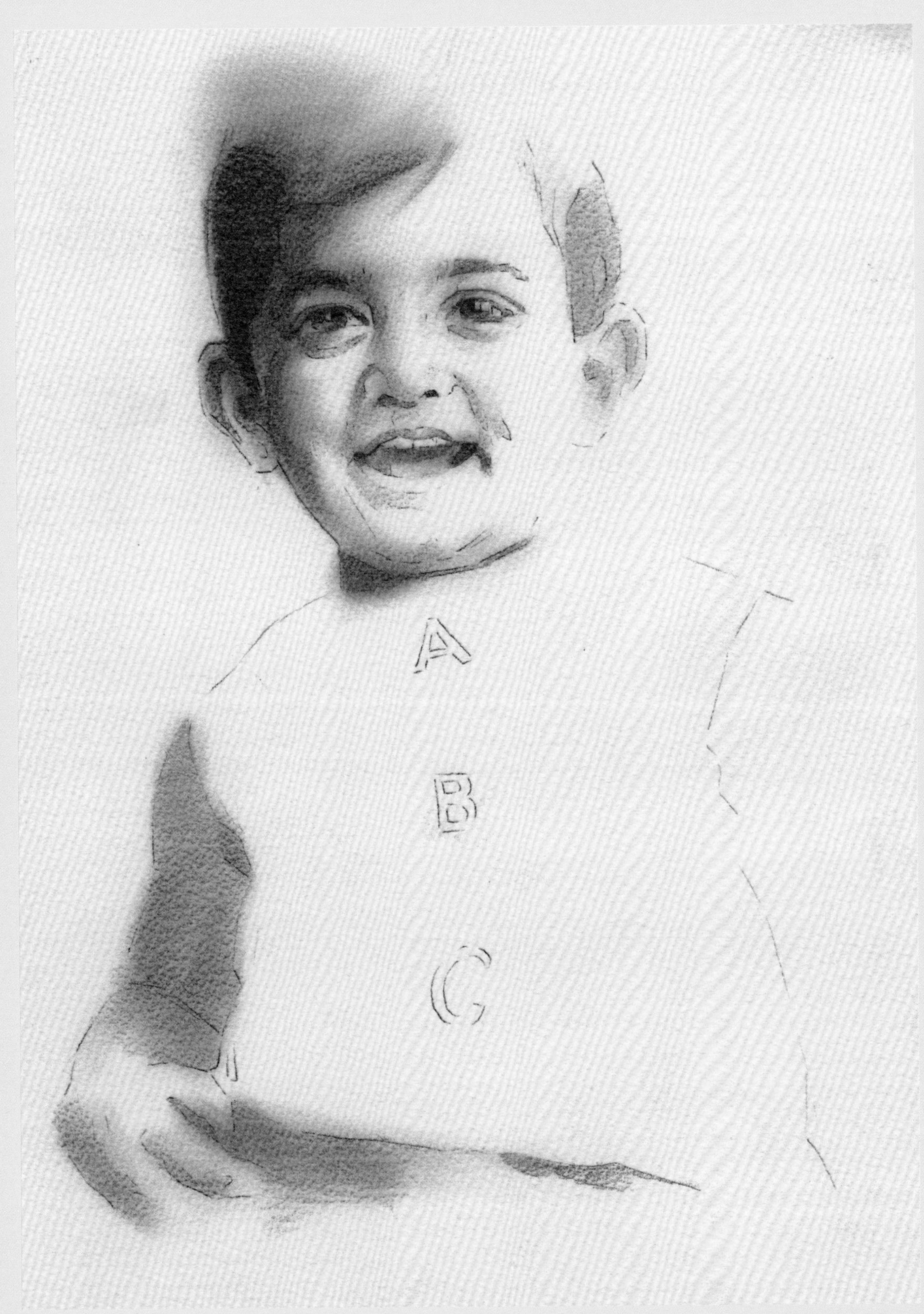

A smiling and cheerful sketch of Aamir as a child.

Young Aamir with his mother Zeenat Hussain.

Facing page: Maulana Abul Kalam Azad was the great-granduncle of Aamir Khan.

Khan, after his great-granduncle, proves this. As a commitment towards his roots and family, the actor did something very special to celebrate his sister Nikhat's 50th birthday. He gave a priceless gift to her; copies of five speeches of Maulana sahab, which he sourced from the National Archives of India. This was the first time that his siblings heard Maulana sahab's voice, which inevitably left them teary eyed; all thanks to Aamir, a true family man.

Herat, Afghanistan is the place from where the journey of this charming Khan family started. They have been more active and relatively known for their cinematic side. Aamir's father Tahir Hussain has five brothers and sisters. In an interview in January 2011 to *Open* magazine Aamir once revealed, 'My full name is Mohammed Aamir Hussain Khan.' But for his screen name he opted for 'Aamir Khan', a short and easy one. Being a descendant of the famed Afghani Pathan clan he does show some of the typical Pathani characteristics in his strides. He never shied away from quoting that Khan is the name of the 'tribe' and that he was not very sure of its real origin. He said that all Khans were Pathans, if only their surnames were considered. But since he was neither born in Afghanistan nor did he speak the local language Pashto, he considers himself a typical 'Bandra boy'; born and brought up in Mumbai.

The actor's mother Zeenat was born in Banaras while his father hailed from Bhopal but shifted to Lucknow. Zeenat also came from a film family. The well-known Fazli Brothers were her uncles. Aamir had been in search of his mother's home in Banaras when he was promoting his film *3 Idiots*. He travelled incognito towards Telia Nala, the area where his mother spent the early years of her life. He said once that if he had the time, he would certainly wish to travel back in time to absorb the energy of the mango orchards of his great-grandfather. His paternal ancestral home is in Shahabad, a place near Hardoi in Uttar Pradesh (UP). He has never been there, and never needed to, as his family had moved first to Lucknow and then to Bombay in the late 1940s and 1950s respectively. But the land, which belonged to his great-grandfather has tremendous emotional value for him, thus, he has bought it. Aamir said in an interview in August 2012, 'This was a sentimental decision. I have hardly spent time in Shahabad but it is my ancestral home. And there is a bond. When I heard that some of my cousins wanted to sell their homes because they have moved on in life, I expressed a desire to buy it back from them. I have said it earlier and I am repeating myself that someday I will definitely try out farming. This land is ideal for farming and I want to go to Shahabad and give farming a shot.' Besides Aamir, the land has been registered in the names of his brother

With his uncle Nasir Hussain at the premiere of Jo Jeeta Wohi Sikandar.

Faisal and his two sisters. Confirming this, Aamir said, 'I have done that because I want my siblings to have homes right next to mine. I really don't know when, but the idea is someday I would like all four of us and my mother to spend time together in our ancestral home. Perhaps all my cousins and my nieces and nephews will also join in. It will be the perfect venue for our family reunion.'

Though politics has been a part of his bloodline, the actor was always inclined towards cinema; thanks to his uncle and father who were actively involved in the Hindi film industry since late 1950s. His uncle came to Mumbai from Lucknow, UP in the late forties. With a flair for writing, he was the first one in the family to venture into films. For more than four decades he created rock and roll musical ballads, suspense thrillers, romantic capers and action-packed films. The producer-director had made some outstanding movies in his time and launched many careers, including that of his nephew Aamir. Although he never took credit, his production house had given the industry some of the superstars of that time like Shammi Kapoor and Asha Parekh.

When Nasir sahab launched Aamir, he did an advertising campaign with billboards asking people 'Who is Aamir Khan?' and 'Who is this boy next door?' At that time even he did not know he had a star in his own family. Aamir worked as an assistant in Nasir Hussain Films. Apparently Aamir was always closer to his uncle than his father. He called him *chachajaan*. *Chacha* and *bhatija* shared a special equation with each other. Aamir always considered him his only guru. Once on the eve of Teacher's Day he said, 'My guru was my uncle Nasir (Hussain) sahab, because I worked for four years with him as an assistant director. Even my debut as a child actor was in his film *Yaadon Ki Baaraat*.' Aamir wished that his late uncle would have seen his directorial debut *Taare Zameen Par* (2007). 'I will always regret that when I directed my first film *Taare Zameen Par*, my uncle had passed away. I always feel that if he had been there, he would have been very happy. I always miss him that way.'

Mansoor Khan in his office on Hill Road during the making of Qayamat Se Qayamat Tak *(QSQT).*

Aamir can claim to be self-made but his dynastic influences have contributed a great deal to his personality. The actor-producer has always said that he derives inspiration from people with courage and strength. Thus, in his list of favourites are his uncle, his mother and his cousins Mansoor Khan and Nuzhat. The star shares a special bond with his cousin who launched him in his debut film *Qayamat Se Qayamat Tak* (*QSQT*). As children they were close friends and after growing up the duo also worked together; making films they believed in. Apart from Aamir's first film, they made two more beautiful films *Jo Jeeta Wohi Sikandar* (1992) and *Akele Hum Akele Tum* (1995). They are so close-knit that when Aamir was searching for references for his character in *3 Idiots* he chose to model himself on Pablo, Mansoor's son.

Years back Mansoor shifted his base to Coonoor, where he has been busy farming and doing philanthropic activities. He chose to move away from the mad world of films, of which Aamir is still a part. Aamir has imbibed several values from his uncle, one of which is maintaining his family relations. He walked into the footsteps of his illustrious uncle and launched his nephew Imran Khan, son of Nuzhat. Since Aamir was busy with *Taare Zameen Par*, he enticed Mansoor to return to Mumbai to oversee the production of Imran's debut film *Jaane Tu... Ya Jaane Na* (2007). It was the familial bond they share that drove the reticent Mansoor back to production. Imran represents the next generation of their family who has taken the plunge into films as an actor. The film was received very well at the box-office. Aamir had also taken on the mantle of being an elder in the family and played an instrumental role in organising Imran's wedding ceremony. It is not surprising that Imran is following in the footsteps of his illustrious *mamu* (maternal uncle). Imran looks up to his *mamu* with gratitude for both personal and professional reasons. Life came to a full circle when Aamir's eldest son Junaid decided to continue his father's legacy. He is now assisting writer-director Rajkumar Hirani in his yet to be released film *P.K.*

Aamir's father was born in Bhopal, had his moorings in Lucknow before following his *bade bhaisaab* (elder brother) Nasir to Bombay in 1955. He first started as an assistant to his brother and also acted in a few films. Eventually, he became a producer. Even though Tahir struggled to gain recognition, he successfully launched the careers of stars like Reena Roy, Rakesh Roshan and music director Bappi Lahiri. Rakesh Roshan had once mentioned that Tahir Hussain was one of the most dignified producers in the Hindi film industry. He has shown his gratitude towards him for signing him in *Madhosh* (1974) and *Zakhmee* (1975) during the days when Rakesh was not doing well as an actor. Rakesh believed that Tahir Hussain was responsible for introducing some good actors in the industry. He also gave a break to director Mehul Kumar, who is known for his films like *Krantiveer* (1994) and *Mrityudaata* (1997), by producing his bilingual (Hindi-Gujarati) debut film *Phir Janam Lenge Hum* (1977), which was also called *Janam Janam Na Saath*.

Aamir with his elder sister Nikhat and father Tahir Hussain.

Even though Tahir Hussain only had a moderately successful career, he did produce some remarkable films like *Hum Hain Rahi Pyar Ke* (1993), *Tum Mere Ho* (1990), *Zakhmee* (1975), *Anamika* (1973) and *Caravan* (1971). He loved working with newcomers and made a significant difference to the lives of many people in this industry. One such novice, Anita Raj, who acted in his film *Dulha Bikta Hai* (1982), recalled him as a man of principle. He was one of the earliest producers to address the problem of dowry through cinema. His sincerity in making this film was applauded by making the film tax-free. Aamir has inculcated this great quality from his father. As a producer Tahir Hussain gained tremendous goodwill in the film industry. When he breathed his last on 2 February 2010, many mourners including the old-timers who had worked with him, gathered to pay homage. Clearly they had not forgotten that he was a visionary in his own right. On this occasion of bereavement, Asha Parekh who was his brother's muse said about him, 'He was a very nice person

Tahir Hussain sharing a joke with son Aamir at their Bandra residence.

and had a great sense of humour. I did three films with him—*Caravan*, *Hamara Khandaan* and *Zakhmee*. He had also acted with me in *Dil Deke Dekho*. I had a long association with him and had attended his wedding and have seen his children grow up. He was also a partner with us in our distribution business called Movie Gem.' The highs and lows in his career became a template for his son.

Aamir reminisces with sadness the time when his father used to make films. He does not hesitate to accept that his father was not a very successful producer-director like his uncle. Tahir Hussain toiled a lot to procure finances for his films. The stars during those days always troubled him for dates and money. When his films failed, creditors landed up at his doorstep demanding back their money. All these incidents had an immense impact on little Aamir's mind. He recollects that more than six to seven times Faisal and his name appeared on the school notice board for non-payment of fees. All the while, his mother suffered quietly. She stitched their school uniforms three times of their current size, so that they would last longer. Aamir knows the perils of being a producer who fought hard to meet personal and professional ends. He cites his father's tussle when he is asked as to why he took so long to become a producer himself. In an interview to *t2*, a supplement of *The Telegraph* in 2011, Aamir said, 'It was a difficult decision to make. Having watched my father as a producer, I had decided to only act in films and never ever produce movies. So, if you happen to get hold of any of my early interviews, you will find me saying that I never wanted to produce films.' Aamir explained, 'It was not that my father wasn't successful as a producer. He did produce films like *Caravan* and *Anamika* and *Locket*. The films were successful but since my father wasn't a hardcore businessman, he never really made the kind of money he could have made. He loved making films and was a very brave producer. He gave breaks to a lot of talent ... But he wasn't a sharp businessman and was financially never on top.' The actor mentioned once, 'It's a thankless job because after employing an entire unit you get all the brickbats for things going wrong; and when the film becomes a hit, the creative talent gets all the credit, never the producer.' 'The reality is,' he added, 'that if it hadn't been for the producer, the creative talent would not have got an opportunity.'

Bound by the sentiments he has for his father, the actor bought all the perpetual rights of his father's films and gifted them to his mother who was the sole and silent witness to her husband's difficulties. It is now her only connection with her late husband. It took a while for him to procure those eleven films. When Aamir wanted to buy back all the films his father had produced, he asked Jayantilal Gada, CMD, Pen India to help him out. Tahir Hussain had mortgaged the negatives with the Hindujas and could not take them back. The Hindujas had sold the rights to Shemaroo who have a library of over 400 films with them. Jayantilal met Raman Maroo of Shemaroo who was his friend and requested him to give back the rights to Aamir. Initially they were a bit hesitant but later Shemaroo were kind enough to return all the films to Aamir at the same price at which they had bought it from the Hindujas. Ultimately, an emotional wish of a son who had lost his father was fulfilled. The films are now a part of the library of Aamir Khan Productions. Tahir Hussain's strife had a tremendous impact on his son and what he is today is partly a result of this.

Today, Aamir's responses to issues reflect on many problems his family had suffered. He was exposed to the uncertainties of film business right from his childhood. He once mentioned that his father never wanted his children to be in films. Aamir recollected that his father's film *Locket* starring Jeetendra and Rekha was stalled due to multiple reasons. For nearly five years, the financiers called up daily to recover their funds. Their family life was disturbed too. He also revealed that once his father woke up at midnight and frantically started searching for his graduation certificate. He thought

Above: With Jayantilal Gada.

Facing page: Aamir with his son Azad Rao Khan at Mumbai airport.

that getting a job would be the only way to support his family. His father was completely bankrupt in the 1980s and those times are clearly etched in Aamir's memory. For a long time there was nothing to do for him and it was quite understandable that he did not want the uncertain life of the film industry to affect his children.

Reena Dutta (extreme left) with friends and Kiran Rao with Azad.

Facing page: Aamir (left) and daughter Ira (right; with a bag in hand) at a football match.

Cinema was Tahir Hussain's soul and his destiny gave him another lease of life as a producer-director. He bounced back with a film *Tum Mere Ho* in 1990 starring his son Aamir and Juhi Chawla. The film did not do very well at the box-office, but it certainly gave him confidence to return to production. It was later in 1993, that his next venture *Hum Hain Rahi Pyar Ke*, with the same lead pair directed by Mahesh Bhatt released and became a super hit. Juhi remembers him with warmth. Offering her condolences, she mentioned that he was like a father figure to her and made her feel like part of the family when she was a newcomer.

In his seventies, Aamir's father saw his son's success as an actor. He was proud of his son. He passed away due to a cardiac arrest when Aamir was on an overseas trip. He will always be remembered and respected for his honesty and principles; the attributes that are also noticeable in his superstar son. Being the elder son he has taken responsibility of steering the family. Aamir has three children—a son Junaid and a daughter Ira from his first wife Reena Dutta and son Azad from his second wife Kiran Rao. He continues to live in Mumbai with Kiran and Azad. To sometimes give him company he has his father's memories and a bank of films that he had made in the times gone by.

birth of aamir hussain khan

Yaadon ki baaraat nikli hai
aaj dil ke dwaare
Dil ke dwaare
Sapnon ki shehnai beete
dino ko pukare
Dil ke dwaare...

This song from the movie *Yaadon Ki Baaraat*, in which child actor Aamir starred, talks of old childhood memories and dreams. Childhood dreams have an innocence, which cannot be compared with the fancies of adulthood. Such thoughts are more rooted to a childish belief that disappears with the passage of time. There are three qualities that stand out in the life of this extraordinary man. First, is his need to acquire an in-depth knowledge of whatever he undertakes to participate in. Second, is to stick to his principles even if a decision he has made goes wrong. Third, but most important, is his loyalty towards his friends and his commitment towards family responsibilities. For him, life was not just about achieving good grades and compliments from teachers but much more.

Aamir in a discussion with his father at their Bandra home.

Though Aamir's life as a cute, vibrant child has already been packaged well on the silver screen there is much to learn about his childhood. His uncle perhaps secretly knew the destiny of his charismatic little nephew. The die was cast. The kid was introduced by his uncle as a child artiste in a very small role in the hit, action-packed drama *Yaadon Ki Baaraat*, which released in 1973. This Dharmendra starrer was known for its musical numbers and its title song became an instantly popular among the masses.

Though films, script readings, story narrations were a part of everyday household activities for his family, eight was too small an age for Aamir to know if adulation was what he wanted in his life. He was a different child, one who was both sensitive and observant. He cried easily while watching movies or reading books. The first film that he saw was a Laurel and Hardy film, which brought him to tears. Though it was a funny film, the child was petrified that the characters may get caught due to their mischievous activities. Aamir, who loves his brother Faisal dearly, actually bawled while watching his baby brother caught in a fire in a scene from *Pyar Ka Mausam*

and had to be taken out of the cinema hall. He never forgets anything which has touched an emotional chord within him at some point. He even remembered how deeply he was moved when he saw a street boy share the little food he had collected with another younger child. His attention to detail is apparent in the work he engages in. Decades later, when Aamir had a near perfect directorial debut *Taare Zameen Par* it did not surprise anyone. But before proceeding further, let us go into flashback mode and find out what his upbringing and youth was all about.

Being the son of a film producer, Aamir had seen his family's resources ebb and flow with every box-office hit and flop. Early in life he reconciled himself to the irregular lifestyle that came with jolts and jubilations—sometimes with perks and sometimes with penury! But along with this he acquired the tenacity that over a period of time has become a characteristic of his life. Born on 14 March 1965, Aamir was a lovable, chubby kid with fair complexion and grew up in a neighbourhood inhabited by the notable people of the film industry.

Even before the actor's birth, his father had chosen a name for him. He had decided to name his second child 'Aamir'—a leader, someone who would achieve tremendous success in whatever he does. He was a shy child with a mind of his own. Being close to his mother, the child was nurtured with independent ideals. She remembers him as a kid who always preferred to tie his own shoelaces and button his shirt rather than take help—quite different from kids who troubled their parents to do every little thing for them—even if that meant an unkempt look. Even as a four-year-old, the little boy could differentiate between what was worthy and what was not. Aamir once mentioned in his speech, which he delivered while felicitating actor Dev Anand at a function held in Y.B. Chavan Centre, Mumbai that one day when his mother noticed that his shoelaces were tied properly and his shirt was tucked in, she instantly knew that he had seen Dev Anand's film.

As a child, Aamir had shown streaks of having an exceptional personality. The kid was not very friendly with outsiders, but was extremely carefree and

A shot from Aamir's directorial debut, Taare Zameen Par.

Facing page: Aamir felicitating actor Dev Anand at a function held in Y.B. Chavan Centre, Mumbai.

shared a good bond with his cousins, brothers and sisters. His mother Zeenat remembers her eldest son dominating almost every family conversation and he was also capable of bullying others! The child has his own way of getting things done while being witty and smart too. Younger brother Faisal and sister Farhat used to run errands for their big brother till they realised that they were being conned. More of such incidences have been revealed about his days as a child by his mother. He would sit for hours with a stock of jam sandwiches and read comics in his bedroom. He would very sweetly tell his kid brother and sister to fetch water for him by pitching one against the other. By the time the two siblings became aware that they were merely being used as water carriers, Aamir would come up with another conjuring trick to make them listen to him and run more errands.

With Saina Nehwal, playing a game of badminton at Khar Gymkhana.

Tahir Hussain too shared some interesting information about his son's hobbies as a kid. Tahir spoke about his son's immense love for tennis and that at one point of time everyone thought Aamir would become a professional player. Aamir used to play five hours in a day at the Khar Gymkhana. He had also travelled all over from Kolhapur to Pune, shared rooms in lodges with several other players and had won the state championship for tennis in the under-fourteen category. His father was of the opinion that his tennis was adversely affecting his grades in school and asked him to give up tennis. 'My marks (in academics) stayed where they were but my tennis stopped,' recalled Aamir. He has several fond remembrances of those days. Once when Aamir had come home victorious from a tennis match his mother asked him if he had won or lost. As his game was always better than others, he had naturally won. But when his mother enquired about the boy who lost, it set Aamir thinking. He had never thought from that perspective ever. This changed his mindset and made him realise that there are always various facets of every situation. Now he always makes it a point to think about situations from other people's outlook as well.

He has an insatiable desire to develop his skills with complete focus. As a teenager the actor excelled in every field that interested him. His father knew that no matter what his own fortunes were, his elder son had the capacity to fare better in life than him. His mother can recall only one occasion when he had to face failure. It was a hilarious incident; a three-year-old Aamir participated in a race and some parents from his neighbourhood came to encourage him on the field. They cheered him on, 'C'mon Aamir!' He thought that they were calling him back and left the race assuming that he should not disrespect his elders. By that time the race got over and he became furious. He had lost his concentration and the race. He could not forgive his neighbours for that!

Childhood threw open another facet of this star-to-be. His maternal grand-aunt Zohra Begum had noticed his popularity among the girls. In fact Aamir was admitted to the nearby school—the Avabai Petit Girls' High School, which shared the boundary wall of Marina Apartments, where he still lives. Although it was strictly a girls' school they admitted boys in the nursery. His elder sister Nikhat was already going to the same school. Though Aamir was a shy boy, still he was very comfortable with the girls in his class. Zohra Begum started calling him *kanhaiya lal* who brought home many *gopis*! Aamir eventually got admission in St. Anne's School, which was on the other side of the Pali Hill. It is interesting to note that even as a kid he always tried to prove his point to fellow students. Even today the actor is known for getting his point across, no matter what the situation is.

Another admirable trait in him is his respect for elders in his family and neighbourhood. His mother remembers her son growing up as an argumentative child, but his arguments were restricted to his peers. He always knew how to behave well with elders. He never crossed his line and thus, never gave anyone an opportunity to reprimand him. But there too were times when he stood his ground to prove his point.

Aamir was an attractive kid. Although he was seen on screen for the first time in *Yaadon Ki Baaraat*, the first offer he got was to play the part of young Shashi Kapoor in *Pyar Ka Mausam*. Strangely, he refused the offer! His uncle Nasir had asked his sister-in-law to dress the child and bring him on the sets. Aamir did go for the shoot, but refused to be a part of the particular shot. He was required to sit in a car. He did not sit inside the car because it did not belong to his friend Reena Khosla, the daughter of another film producer Raj Khosla. She lived in the same building, was his close childhood friend and he would not sit in anybody else's car but hers. Throughout the day everyone coaxed him to sit in the car, but the reluctant kid was adamant. Since the shot had to be taken, his younger brother Faisal acted in his place. This incident clearly shows that even as a child he was clear about his loyalties towards his friends. Till today this aspect in him is apparent in all the relationships

Aamir with his former wife, Reena Dutta.

he shares within and outside the industry. No wonder the 'Time-Pass Gang' he introduced long back still cherishes the lovely memories of what they did as kids in the building complex. They used to organise a fete every year and Aamir was naturally the leader. As the fete grew popular, kids of other buildings were also allowed admission to it on an entry ticket to enjoy the stalls and games.

As a child, Aamir had the habit of saving the money he received on Eid or special occasions like birthdays. He used to deposit it all with his grand-aunt. One day he asked her to give him all the money. The kid wanted to give it to someone the family knew very well. When mother Zeenat came to know of this, she felt very proud that her child has imbibed the right values.

Aamir also loved other games like chess, a game he excels at even today. During his growing years, the Rubik's Cube was a huge challenge for him. The smart lad often cracked it and then went a step further; he wanted to be the fastest to do it. His sister Farhat used to be the timekeeper while he was practising. When she was bored with keeping time, he promised her due acknowledgement if he could break the world record and then she too could become a part of the victory. She agreed and got conned by her sweet brother as usual.

Teenage years

As Aamir grew into a fine boy, his peers began to admire him and started looking up to him. The teenage boy never thought twice before standing up for his brother or friends if they were wronged. He could pick up a fight with anyone and would also win it, such was his determination. When he cleared the 12th grade, he decided to quit studies and join films. He naturally met with opposition at home. As he was obedient to his elders, it was a challenge for him to circumvent a major decision. By being polite and determined about his decision he found his way with his parents. He made them realise that his heart was set to join the Film and Television Institute of India, Pune. If his parents had been adamant he would have obeyed them as a mark of respect. But his mother spoke on his behalf and got his father to agree to let Aamir drop out of college.

Aamir and Juhi Chawla in a scene from the iconic Qayamat Se Qayamat Tak *(*QSQT*).*

He grabbed the first offer he got. He had to face the camera for a short film called *Paranoia* directed by Aditya Bhattacharya. Aditya was legendary director Bimal Roy's grandson and director Basu Bhattacharya's son. His friends like Neena Gupta, Victor Banerjee, Deepa Lagoo and Aamir Khan starred in the film. In an interview given in January 2010 to *India Today* magazine, Aamir recalled, 'I was 16 when I realised I wanted to be an actor. My school friend Aditya Bhattacharya decided to cast me in a 40-minute silent film called *Paranoia*, financed with Rs 8,000 from actor Shreeram Lagoo. Making that film convinced me that this is where I belonged...' It was in this film that actor Shabana Azmi saw him perform and mentioned his prowess as an actor to his parents. All hell broke loose in his house, but Aamir could not lose his focus. His life took another major turn when he got to know that Ketan Mehta was scouting for actors for his film *Holi*. He required some students. Aamir and Ashutosh Gowariker (the writer-director of *Lagaan*) auditioned for this project, and got selected. The shooting was held in Pune for which Aamir had to take his father's approval. As the film was to be shot during his vacations, he got permission easily. After this he also acted in Aditya Bhattacharya's *Raakh*, where he played a negative character. Without much propelling, the actor's destiny was being shaped. The teenager blossomed into a fine artiste. Aamir had also started assisting his uncle Nasir in his films; an experience that would later hold him in good stead. Then one fine day, his uncle decided to speak to his parents about his plans for Aamir. He expressed his utmost desire to launch Aamir in his upcoming film as the lead actor. Aamir's fate had been tied to the movie industry. In 1988, at the young age of twenty-three, he played the main lead in the iconic film *Qayamat Se Qayamat Tak* (*QSQT*).

Back then he had never dreamt of starting his own production company and becoming a success. Though with *Qayamat Se Qayamat Tak*, the momentous trip towards superstardom of a thorough professional and a thinking actor had begun.

QSQT

LAUNCHING OF THE BOY NEXT DOOR

'I was a rebel of sorts. I did go against the current. When I passed the 12th standard, I quit studies. Everyone advised me against that ... Looking back, I am happy with my decision.'

Mansoor Khan (extreme left), Aamir and Nasir Hussain during the shooting of Qayamat Se Qayamat Tak *(*QSQT*).*

Facing page: An intense looking Aamir at a special photo shoot for Ghulam.

The late 1980s saw a slew of films that were high on violence and less on content. Romance had almost taken a back seat during this period. Nasir Hussain who had been known for making light entertainers was reaching his nadir as a filmmaker. For the first time his films like *Manzil Manzil* and *Zamaane Ko Dikhana Hai* failed at the box-office. Though the filmmaker had not yet given up on his trademark musical films he knew that the audience had changed. This was also the time when videocassettes started flourishing. He needed to bring a radically different perspective to regain his stature and to be in step with this new age. The need of the hour was to reinvent his cinema to bring the audience back to the theatres. Like Raj Kapoor made *Bobby*, Nasir started toying with the idea of making a film with fresh faces. Though it was a formidable challenge, the whole idea was to lure people back into the darkness of theatres rather than watch videocassettes at home. He also recognised the requirement to bring back quality into the stories. The heroes needed to be real and not imaginary.

Javed Akhtar suggested to Nasir sahab that Aamir be cast as the hero in Qayamat Se Qayamat Tak.

At that time Nasir sahab's son, Mansoor Khan, was busy writing the script of *Jo Jeeta Wohi Sikandar*, which he wanted to produce and direct. He felt it would interest the young generation. He sensed that people were getting tired of watching the monotonous masala films, full of action that featured angry heroes seeking revenge. Mansoor was keen on making the kind of cinema he believed in and did not show much interest when his father asked him to add a different angle to his story. After all, it was his chance to showcase his talent as a writer and a visionary to the next-gen cinemagoers. After pondering for some time, he sensed a need to revamp the old storyline and decided to consider his father's suggestions. Along with his cousins, he tweaked the script and between Mansoor, Nuzhat and Aamir a new story took shape. The cousins never even realised that they were writing a path-breaking film.

The year was 1987. Nasir Hussain was auditioning for his new production and was on the lookout for a fresh lead pair. When nothing was working out, apparently lyricist Javed Akhtar's suggestion rang some bells in his head. Akhtar on noticing the intelligent and good-looking face of Nasir sahab's efficient young assistant Aamir said, 'You have a hero at home. Why venture out!' The veteran director then decided to introduce his nephew as the lead actor in his ambitious project *Qayamat Se Qayamat Tak* (*QSQT*).

Aamir was not sure if things would work out and his dream of becoming a Hindi film hero will ever come true. Thus, when his uncle first told him that he wanted him to act in this love story he was making, Aamir did not believe him until he began working on the script. But his *chachajaan* was sure that he had found his hero in Aamir who would one day become a star. He took permission from Aamir's parents and signed him on for the film. Initially, Nasir sahab wanted to direct the film, but due to his failing health the responsibility of direction and production was handed over to his son Mansoor.

Aamir and Juhi, the fresh lead pair, in a scene from Qayamat Se Qayamat Tak.

During the making of the film none of them knew what its fate would be at the box-office. The movie was launching several careers: musicians Anand-Milind, singers Udit Narayan and Alka Yagnik, and actor Juhi Chawla. She had starred in a flop film called *Sultanat* prior to this. The film was also introducing Aamir Khan and not to forget, director Mansoor Khan. While others were new to Mansoor, he had directed Juhi in a shampoo advertisement for his company Scan Media. Meanwhile, she had got an offer to play Draupadi in B.R. Chopra's *Mahabharat*. She had almost agreed when Mansoor approached her for the lead role in his film. She took permission from the Chopras and agreed to the offer made by Mansoor.

In a film still from Dil.

Aamir vividly recalls the first-ever shot he gave for the film on an outdoor location. He reminisced, 'I remember when we began shooting it was early in the morning in Ooty on a hilltop and between trees. The first couple of takes happened and we still hadn't got the shot and then suddenly this fog spread. Of course, we had to wait for the fog to clear, but the fog stayed for something like eight hours. As it was too late and everybody was tired, the shoot for the day was cancelled.' This was one of the minor obstacles they faced and there were many more waiting befall them.

Juhi at a special photo shoot.

Juhi recalled her first scene that was shot at Essel Studios, 'First day of shooting—I'm sitting with my dadi. I don't remember the dialogues but I remember the setting. I'm wearing a ghagra-choli with a big, long wig of flowing hair. And pink and blue eye shadow. Finally when I watched the film, even I was aghast *ki yeh sab kya hum log karte the*?' [Did we actually do all these things during the making of the movie?]

Aamir has some affectionate memories of working with Juhi in *Qayamat Se Qayamat Tak*, 'Juhi was great to work with. She is a wonderful actress. In fact I have always felt that she was much better than me. Honestly, I felt her performance was superior. She was a lot more comfortable as a performer and in front of the camera. I wasn't. I was awkward. I would look at her and say, "Hmm ... I wish I could give a shot like this".'

Juhi narrated her experience of working with Aamir, 'For a while we worked together. *Ek toh dono* newcomer *the, ek dum darr nahin tha ek dusre se* [We were both newcomers and not scared of each other]. I came to this atmosphere where everybody was young and new, *toh lagta tha ki arre apne* college friend *ke saath abhi* acting *karni hai* [It was new to me and I felt that I had to shoot with my college friend]. We were such good friends that if I felt awkward I could tell him, if he wasn't getting something right ... *Main bada apna* suggestion *bhi de sakti thi* [I could offer my suggestions to Aamir]. It was totally one on one.'

On seeing the film's trial critics expressed their dissatisfaction. The film was shown to several distributors and had trial runs for the media. But the reports were not too flattering. Anand Shrivastav of the music director duo Anand-Milind recalled in an interview given to *Filmfare* in 2012, 'Ironically, the music wasn't appreciated during the distributor trials. The film had no buyers. They told director Mansoor Khan that they would invest their money, only if he changed the music and the tragic ending. But Mansoor stuck to his guns and the gamble paid off...' After seeing the film's trial, eminent music director R.D. Burman predicted a bright future for Aamir. He prophesied that the star, the film and the music would reach phenomenal heights. But as most of the responses by the industry veterans were not very positive, the producers had to think of ways to attract the audiences to the theatres. They knew they had to market the film in a big way to the people.

With Juhi in a sad and emotional scene from Hum Hain Rahi Pyar Ke.

In an interview to *The Illustrated Weekly of India* in January 1991, Aamir said, 'When Mansoor and I saw the film run in trials, we ran into depression. The mistakes would stare at us. I remember goading my uncle to promote the film much more than he was already doing. We thought we had mucked up the film.' To popularise the film, Aamir and Juhi themselves spent days, urging taxi and auto-rickshaw drivers to carry their film stickers on their vehicles. Juhi fondly recollects, 'During those times, we used to have stickers. Some car stickers promoting the movie. *Toh apni gaadi pe chipka diya. Phir toh* literally *mere* building *ke neeche main aur ghar ke koi ek do jan ko pakadke jaati thi aur* taxi driver *ko jaake bolti ki*, "please *main yeh* taxi *pe laga dun?" Toh koi toh bolta tha*, "*Aye kaun hai yeh? Hatt!*" (*laughs*) *aur koi* "*Haan haan laga do*." And then auto *pe lagate the hum log* and it was so nice because it's something I never did again in my whole life. But at that time *Ek bhi lag jaye na* ... maybe *koi dekhke humko* picture *dekhne aa jayega*' [I would put stickers promoting the movie on not only my car, but also on cabs and autos if they permitted us, thinking that such publicity would at least draw some people to watch us in the theatres].

Ready to be clicked after the film screening of Qayamat Se Qayamat Tak *in 2013 when it completed 25 years.*

Aamir mentioned about his launch pad in an interview, 'It was *chachajaan* who came up with the idea of having a hoarding with the hero of the film standing with glares covering his eyes. The hoarding screamed, "Who is Aamir Khan?" That set the ball rolling. The next series of hoardings screamed, "Ask the girls next door!"' Naturally, almost everyone was now vaguely interested in the larger-than-life billboards with this mysterious guy looking upwards. With this curiosity the film was released in the theatres.

When released, the film was slow in its collections. Aamir gave the figures, 'The first week collections were 88%, the second week it slumped to 82%; the third week it went further down to 79% or 76% ... It kept going down. And then the fourth week it rose to 96%! It suddenly jumped in the fourth week because in the

Aamir's piercing gaze in a still from Raakh.

first 2-3 weeks, by word of mouth the news spread that it was a great film.' It created a euphoria that only Raj Kapoor's *Bobby* had created when it was released in 1973. Clearly the public verdict showed that it was time for a huge change in the kind of films that would now be made. *Qayamat Se Qayamat Tak* turned out to be the game changer. It also brought back the audience to the theatres. Romance returned to films once again. The film's long title led to it being popularly referred to by the acronym *QSQT*. Even this sparked off a fad in Hindi movies, with very long titles being promoted by their shortened substitutes like *DDLJ* for *Dilwale Dulhania Le Jayenge* and *HAHK* for *Hum Aapke Hain Koun..!*

In another interview Aamir said, 'It was a very fresh film; it was appealing to a family audience, to young people. It was a new language in cinema. It was a new kind of making films. So it really appealed to that audience, which had actually stopped going to theatres. The film went on to be hugely successful and I was an overnight star.' The distributors in Bombay decided to use the situation further in their favour by introducing a new strategy of buying eight or more tickets of the film and getting a poster/photo of Aamir Khan and Juhi Chawla absolutely free. This plan worked and the collections of the film showed a big jump.

With this film's success, Aamir became the reigning heart-throb of the country and Juhi became everybody's darling. Aamir was amused by the adulation he was receiving. He was inundated with calls from girls and fan mails. While many girls called to tell him that they loved him in the film, some even landed up at his house and asked him out. Juhi was getting over a 100 letters every day. As instructed by her parents, she replied to most of her fan mails personally. Juhi said her parents were of the opinion, '"These are your first fans" and I guess they just were so overwhelmed that when anybody would write nice things to me, they were like, "answer it".'

Wandering pensively in the compound of his home.

People were recognising Aamir everywhere. The debutante actor said in one of his numerous media interactions, 'I remember driving my uncle's car. At the traffic signal, I happened to look in the adjoining car casually and the people inside were smiling and waving. I wondered, "How do I know these people? Who are they? Why are they smiling at me? Must be my uncle's friends or my dad's friends?" So I returned the smile because I thought I'm supposed to know them. After a while it struck me! These people were trying to figure out if I am the person who starred

in *QSQT*? That confusion went on for a while and then I realised that actually they had seen the film and they recognised me and that's why...'

Conversing with his former wife at a public function.

Facing page: Aamir and Pooja Bhatt with director Mahesh Bhatt during the shoot of Dil Hai Ke Manta Nahin.

During the filming of *Qayamat Se Qayamat Tak*, Aamir got married to Reena Dutta, his childhood sweetheart but had to keep his marriage a secret for three weeks on his uncle's request. As many newcomers were starting their careers with this film, for their sake and his, Aamir had to keep this news under wraps for some time. Several years after the film's release, Aamir's nephew, Imran Khan in an interview to *Filmfare* in 2010 revealed, 'Aamir agreed and the day the movie was declared a hit, he went to my granddad and said, "*Chachajaan*, there is no more risk to anyone's career and I would like to tell the truth".' 'It was quite a journey,' Aamir affectionately stated.

Not only Aamir and Juhi, it was actually overnight stardom for everyone associated with the film. Mansoor took the biggest risk of ending the film on a sad note. He explained the reasons for changing the entire track and introducing the sad ending stating, 'For me it was always a tragic ending because the premise was so strong and difficult that I couldn't see the two families getting together. My father would always insist saying that sad endings don't work. People don't like to cry. They're already crying in their lives anyway.' But soon the tragic, romantic love story became a cult film.

All odds worked in their favour or should we say the *Qayamat Se Qayamat Tak* team turned them in their favour with the sheer belief they had in their work and the determination to carve a new approach to making films. Recently, the super hit movie completed its silver jubilee year on 29 April 2013. To celebrate the success, Aamir held a press conference at Film City earlier that day where he cut a cake and sang the lines of the nostalgic song, '*Papa Kehte Hain...*' He later held a special screening of the film at Light Box Theatre in Mumbai. It was followed by a party

Clockwise from extreme left: The QSQT *group—singers Alka Yagnik (extreme left), music composers Anand-Milind and Udit Narayan (extreme right) with Aamir and Kiran celebrating the film's silver jubilee; A special cake was also cut at a media meet in Film City, Mumbai on the occasion; The* mahurat *shot from the film* Qayamat Se Qayamat Tak *with Tahir Hussain (extreme left) and Nasir Hussain (extreme right).*

Facing page: Juhi and Aamir during the celebrations of QSQT *completing 25 years.*

at Nasir Hussain's bungalow where his grandson Imran Khan resides today. The evening witnessed the presence of the entire cast and crew including Juhi Chawla, Mansoor Khan, Anand-Milind, Udit Narayan, Makrand Deshpande, Alka Yagnik, Asha Sharma, Nandita Thakur, Shiva Rindani, Shehzad Khan and Raj Zutshi among many more.

In the 100 years of Indian cinema, *Qayamat Se Qayamat Tak* is considered among one of the greatest films. Also, with this film a complete entertainer was born on celluloid and an actor who would take the Hindi film industry by storm.

making of a complete entertainer

'Filmmaking is like war. You have to lead from the front.'

today Aamir Khan is known for his high-octane performances in most of his films. He has a rule of thumb, of doing 'one film at a time'. He has adopted this style after learning a lesson from his past failures. This new mantra is working well for him. Though it takes high willpower to resist the lure of lucre, it has never been a problem for Aamir as he has long decided to move out of the mindless mayhem of the mainstream extravaganza. Aamir does not merely 'exist', he 'lives' on his own terms in this industry. This rare individuality of his has won him millions of admirers. People love him not because he is cool, charming or is the sexiest male, but because they associate Aamir with quality cinema and always find substance in his films.

Being a part of the industry for more than twenty-seven years, the performer is admired for the calculated decisions he takes as a producer, director and actor (though not necessarily in that order!). The trajectory of his work has encompassed all the facets of the gruelling film industry. From being a

A film still from Mann.

child artiste to a teenage, rookie assistant in his uncle's production house, a romantic hero to a producer and director, Aamir has dabbled in all the departments successfully. Now, he has also become a television anchor.

Nonetheless, it has never been a smooth ride for Aamir. The journey of this complete entertainer—as an actor, a producer and a director—has been peppered with several ups and downs. While working and understanding the various departments he now excels in, he encountered numerous difficulties, emotional moments, triumphs and tragedies. Every experience in each phase has been a motivating factor in his endeavour for achieving excellence in whatever he does. It is a tale that speaks of this extraordinary man's prerequisite to rise above his circumstances to alter his destiny and become the first amongst equals.

No wonder people call him a perfectionist. He does not agree with the title at all and said that the media gave it to him. Aamir in an interview once said, 'I feel there is no such thing as perfection, especially in a creative field like cinema. There's no correct way of doing things in a creative field. We are all artistes expressing ourselves.' He added, 'It's become such a big joke in the family now, that my sister bought me a T-shirt with "Mr Perfect" written on it! However, I agree that I leave no stone unturned in trying to achieve the true potential of the film that we are setting out to make. I am always driven by passion.'

The early phase

Even though Aamir belonged to a film producer's family, his life was still a tough one. He was not born with a golden spoon in his mouth. Considering their circumstances, his father Tahir Hussain had already decided that his children would not live the same unpredictable life like him and hence will not join the film industry. A small role in his uncle's film was acceptable but not a full-fledged occupation as an actor. Tahir Hussain had once mentioned, 'We knew (when he was child) he would excel in anything he did.' But would he also excel as an actor? If Tahir wanted things his way, then Aamir would have to follow. But, destiny had other plans in store for Aamir.

While Aamir was exploring the outside world, his mind was expanding its horizons. He was exposed to extracurricular activities such as dramatics in the 12th standard at Narsee Monjee College, Juhu, Mumbai. During that time, filmmaker Ketan Mehta was on the lookout for fresh talent for his film *Holi* (1984). He called some students for audition and handpicked Ashutosh Gowariker, Aamir Khan and some other boys. Ketan Mehta had seen Aamir's work and wanted him as the protagonist of his film. However, the role went to Ashutosh as Aamir for some reason had shaved off his head. Aamir was cast in the character of Madan Sharma for the film. But before the prodigal son could face the camera, he had to take his father's permission. Since the film was being shot in Pune during his college vacations and his studies would not be affected, he was allowed to go. After the film and particularly his performance received appreciation, he decided to take his family for a preview. His family was shocked and were brutal in

Aamir passionately embracing Karisma Kapoor in a scene from Raja Hindustani.

their reaction, which hit Aamir like a lash. He thought that since they were so accustomed to watching him as a simple boy at home, they must have really felt awkward seeing him in the character of a bald man.

In those days, among his friend circle, becoming a director and joining a film institute was a fad. Being close to his mother, Aamir told her of his desire to join the Film and Television Institute of India at Pune. She knew that his father would immediately turn down the very idea. The worst was, Aamir decided not to study after 12th standard. He knew that becoming a graduate would not help him in the profession he has chosen for himself. When Zeenat broached the subject to her husband, initially he was reluctant, but on second thoughts he said, 'If he wants to join the film industry then it is better that he becomes an assistant in Nasir Hussain Films.' His father believed that in this way he would get a better exposure to production and learn the ropes of direction. Aamir managed to surmount his parental opposition with dexterity. However, the challenge to move forward to make a livelihood in acting was yet to be conquered.

During his vacations he did another film called *Raakh*, which was made by his friend Aditya Bhattacharya. Although this was his first film as an actor, it was released much after his debut film. In 1989, Aamir won his first National Award (Special Jury Award for acting) for the film *Raakh*. Before this, just after his 10th standard, Aamir also did a short 40-minute silent film shot on 16mm called *Paranoia* for Aditya that made him understand the entire process of filmmaking. Aamir was Aditya's helping hand in this project taking on the roles of a spot boy, assistant, production manager and later even as an actor.

The acting phase

Stardom cannot be served on a platter. On receiving accolades for his performance in *Raakh*, Aamir was certain that he was destined to be an actor. However, the journey of becoming a star was not simple. Even after acting in two films, he continued to work as a production assistant with his uncle and was looking for the right opening to showcase his acting talent. The opportunity soon came when the hunt for lively faces began for the banner's new venture *Qayamat Se Qayamat Tak*. When this film released, Aamir Khan's life drastically changed.

He became a much sought after hero. Naturally many producers wanted to cash in on the new lead pair of Aamir-Juhi. Aamir had many producers knocking at his doorstep, and in a frenzy he signed many films without giving it much thought. Soon he became a run-of-the-mill actor, running from one shift to another, shooting for many films and producers at the same time. This went on for around six months. Eventually his films like *Love Love Love* (1989) and *Awwal Number* (1990) started flopping and slowly his magic failed to charm the audience. The initial euphoria of stardom had died. The chocolate boy who melted a million young hearts was now a bitter pill to swallow. With every film of his bombing, reality set in. The bouquets turned into brickbats and the party was over. The number of producers who wanted to sign him waned. But Aamir never passed the buck to anyone for this string of blunders. He knew he was at fault and tried to shoulder the responsibility. In an

Facing page: Dev Anand directing Aamir while shooting for Awwal Number *at the Cricket Club of India.*

interview to *Filmfare*, he acknowledged that as a viewer he didn't quite enjoy some of his films like *Raakh*, *Awwal Number*, *Isi Ka Naam Zindagi* (1992) and *Daulat Ki Jung* (1992). But as he was a part of these films he believes that he should be blamed equally as anyone else involved in these films. In another interview to Shoma Chaudhury of *Tehelka* magazine the actor said, 'When my first film, *QSQT*, was released and became a huge success, there was a lot of pressure on me. The norm was to sign 20-30 films at one time. I ended up signing nine. The directors I liked didn't offer me any films, so I just picked some and took the plunge. When the shoot began, I realised, one, shooting nine films at the same time is bad news, two, the director is the most important aspect of filmmaking.'

While Aamir was cornered and became a victim of the then prevailing system, there were other new heroes who swept the hearts of the audience. Salman Khan arrived with a big bang in 1989 with Rajshri Productions' *Maine Pyar Kiya*. He was an overnight phenomenon. Good love stories were still in vogue and Salman only added to the sparkle. What's more he was not a sweet-looking star like Aamir. He was extremely charming and an action hero. Salman too came from a similar family background as Aamir. His father Salim Khan was the legendary writer of iconic films that starred Amitabh Bachchan and other big actors in the 1970s and 1980s.

Aamir knew very well that to have a sustainable career he needed to get his act right. He learnt it the hard way. He once declared, 'Filmmaking is like war. You have to lead from the front. The director has to be a general ... He has to make you blossom...' But these were the days when his job failed to resurrect. So he took a break to understand what went wrong. He understood that a bad director can mar a good script. It was at this time when Reena, his first wife, stood rock solid by his side.

During the time when Aamir was going through a low point in his profession, another hero started making a mark in films. Shahrukh Khan brought his vibrant energy to the big screen and was emerging as the new star to threaten the reign of even Salman Khan. At that juncture Aamir had decided he would now do films only if his heart was in it and would pay attention to the script as well.

With Farha Naaz (Khan) during the shoot of Isi Ka Naam Zindagi.

In 1990, he got an offer from producer Indra Kumar, who was making a solo hero film called *Dil*, featuring Madhuri Dixit. This film helped Aamir to return to the ranks of the industry's elite. It is still considered as one his best movies by many. Initially Indra was not sure if Aamir would be able to handle certain complicated emotional scenes in the film, but he was glad to observe that Aamir was a fast learner and, thus managed to give an excellent performance. Aamir has very high regard for Indra Kumar as a filmmaker and credits him for saving his career as *Dil* gave Aamir a second lease of life.

However, he skid down again in the number game with two other bad choices following *Dil*—*Deewana Mujh Sa Nahin* (1990) and *Jawani Zindabad* (1990). About *Jawani Zindabad* he recalled in an interview to *The Illustrated Weekly of India*, 'I did not gel well with Farha (Naaz), the lead

Madhuri with Aamir in a romantic scene from Dil.

heroine in the film during its filming. But I had liked the role of the elder brother who shoulders the responsibility of his family. However, I don't think Farha and I as a pair were actually responsible for the movie's poor performance. Technically it could have been a better film.' This experience had made him cautious about the choice of his leading ladies. Later Mahesh

Bhatt wanted to do an adaptation of a Hollywood film with producer Gulshan Kumar. Though Aamir was very keen to work with Mahesh Bhatt his gut feeling was negative about Bhatt's new venture. When Aamir asked his wife for her opinion, she suggested that he should listen to his heart.

Aamir wanted to show that he was not a flash in the pan and so he did meet the maverick director and the producer. Instead, he expressed his desire to do an Indian version of the American romantic comedy film *It Happened One Night*. Mahesh agreed to his idea and named this quirky love story *Dil Hai Ke Manta Nahin*. Soon Aamir was back on the sets with additional confidence. Though this film did not set hearts on fire like his debut film, it did decent business. The songs of the film are hummable even now. Mahesh believes that Aamir has the courage to unlearn and the nerve to constantly renew himself. This quality makes him endearing. On receiving a satisfactory response to this film, Aamir decided to choose his projects even more wisely from then on.

In 1992, among the three films of his that released, *Jo Jeeta Wohi Sikandar* got a better response than the others at the box-office. His cousin Mansoor directed the film. The film went through its share of tragic incidences. Nearly 60–70 per cent of the film had to be reshot and the lead actresses were changed several times for different reasons. All these changes took a toll on Aamir as his role involved scenes with both the girls. 'As an actor, it was the most earth-shattering thing for me because I had given my best and most magical moments the first time,' Aamir recollected. This was just one of the many stumbling blocks he faced when he decided to be choosy. But he was determined to take such problems in his stride. He thoroughly understood that if those carefully picked scripts failed at the box-office it would affect his star rating. But he had faith in himself and was convinced that his decision would pay off one day. And it did, benefitting him and those who supported him.

To secure a top slot as an actor, Aamir had to work his way up like a master chess player. He never denied that he wanted to be the best and was now truly focussed on achieving his dreams. If he could defeat his opponents in tennis and have an upper hand in chess, he was capable of manoeuvring

Aamir at the merchandise launch of Dhoom: 3 *where the game and character dolls were released.*

Facing page: Taking off his T-shirt and cap at the end of a bicycle race held for the promotion of Jo Jeeta Wohi Sikandar.

the course of his acting career too. Now it was a matter of choosing only the best. While other stars were depending on their equation with big banners, Aamir started to move on with a unique strategy like a chess grandmaster to reclaim his lost territory. Aamir did not want to be stuck in the rut of a portraying a chocolate hero on the big screen. He needed to move beyond romancing the heroines behind trees. One way he found was to listen to new scripts from totally new filmmakers who had novel ideas. Meanwhile, he also had to complete the backlog of films he had signed in haste as he did not wish to leave any producer in a lurch.

All these failures taught Aamir many lessons. He would now ask for a total scenario of the movie before even the first shot was taken. As he started moving ahead with renewed determination he knew there would be some face-offs. When Yash Raj Films (YRF) approached him in 1993, he asked for a joint narration, as the project had two heroes in it. The request was refused, so Aamir chose not to do the project. The film was *Darr* (1993). The role eventually went to Shahrukh Khan. The film was a huge hit. But Aamir did not regret his decision of saying no to the project. In the same year he did *Parampara*, directed by Yash Chopra and *Hum Hain Rahi Pyar Ke* (*HHRPK*), directed by Mahesh Bhatt. The latter became a super hit and revived his pairing with Juhi Chawla. The film was based on the 1958 Hollywood romantic comedy *Houseboat* starring Sophia Loren and Cary Grant containing elements of drama and family values in it. Produced by Aamir's father, the film won Tahir Hussain his first *Filmfare* Award in 1994. The leading actress Juhi Chawla received her first *Filmfare* Award that had been eluding her ever since. Despite stiff competition from Meenakshi Sheshadri for *Damini* and Dimple Kapadia for *Rudaali*, Juhi won the *Filmfare* Best Actress Award for her impeccable comic timing and impressive performance in *Hum Hain Rahi Pyar Ke*. Juhi could not believe that this film would win her the award as shooting for it was more like a picnic and moreover comedy was not taken seriously enough in those days.

Success knocks once more

Few people get a second chance to rectify their mistakes and Aamir was lucky to get more than one opportunity. He understood that if he had to remain in the business he would have to redefine himself. What may have worked for others was definitely not working for him: he knew he could not do ten to twelve films at a time like other actors. He had to get completely involved in the projects he was doing.

This period was the turning point in his career and it made him what he is today—a star to reckon with. Aamir Khan also got nicknamed 'interferer'

Seriously discussing the details of a scene with Mahesh Bhatt during the shoot of Dil Hai Ke Manta Nahin.

during this stage in life. However, none of the producers and directors who worked with him agreed to it. He was always disciplined, came to the sets on time, had no starry airs and did what was asked. His brightness was welcomed and so was his punctuality. But what was peculiar were his new demands. He started asking for a bound script of the film before shooting began. He became fastidious about the narrations that he sat for. This period saw the release of his few other notable films. He was paired with Salman Khan for the first time in Rajkumar Santoshi's *Andaz Apna Apna* that released in 1994. The film failed to excite the cinemagoers at that time. These two actors never worked together after that. In a recent interview Aamir stated, '*Andaz Apna Apna* is one my favourite films of all time, it's very close to my heart. Salman is a great person to work with and if we come across a script that excites us, we would be happy to do the film together.' Over a period of time this Rajkumar Santoshi directed comedy turned out to be a masterpiece!

The director's cut!

Talking about directors, it would be interesting to know how they perceived this actor who was now taking interest not only in his own role in the film but also how his co-stars would be placed; how a shot would be taken; how it would affect the shooting and editing of the film. Numerous arguments, debates, ideas and the phrase 'One more shot, sir' were now common on the sets whenever Aamir was shooting. With this newfound approach his career took a significant turn. During those days, Mahesh Bhatt who had offered him a fresh lease of life at the box-office prophesied, 'Aamir will be in the front rows of showbiz in the years to come and become a highly durable commodity.' How true his words were. He said this in January 1991 and today his declaration can be etched in gold. Aamir has given a new meaning to the entertainment industry as he moves from strength to strength. Another director, Rajkumar Santoshi who worked with Aamir in *Andaz Apna Apna* once said, 'Aamir comes on the sets with his own views and not with an attitude. His choice of films reflects this confidence. He offers constructive suggestions and in a few years, I expect Aamir will take up direction.' Mansoor, who may be evasive now, but when he did work with his cousin had said, 'Aamir is a quick learner and he seems to improve day by day. Aamir will overcome the image of a romantic hero and move on to a wider range of characterisation. He has the potential to blend with the background.'

Thereafter, with every film Aamir tried to show a new facet of his in the characters he portrayed. Through the 1990s, the actor signed films like *Afsana Pyar Ka*, *Daulat Ki Jung*, *Isi Ka Naam Zindagi* and *Time Machine* (which got shelved). But in between these duds, he made some interesting choices as well like *Rangeela* (1995), *Akele Hum Akele Tum* (1995), *Raja Hindustani* (1996) and *Ishq* (1997). Each film depicted the talented actor in a different role. He was no longer the chocolate hero romancing heroines. His

Aamir while shooting 'Aati kya Khandala' *from* Ghulam.

Facing page: As Disco Fighter singing 'I hate you (like I love you)' *in* Delhi Belly.

tapori look in *Rangeela* was much appreciated and gave him an edge over his competitors. While Aamir has always been absolutely professional, he also worked in some films made by his friends for personal reasons. He did a film called *Baazi* (1995) with friend Ashutosh Gowariker, whose earlier film *Pehla Nasha* had not been a success. When Ashutosh approached Aamir, he agreed to work in the film opposite Mamta Kulkarni, a fresh face. The film did not do well at the box-office, but he did not lose focus. He continued to be careful about his choice of roles. Still he yet had to match the commercial success of the other two Khans—Salman and Shahrukh. Rather than matching their performances, he opted for a separate route. He diverted his attention to new directors who approached him with contemporary and challenging concepts and even gave successful films one after the other.

In 1998, Mahesh Bhatt signed him on for *Ghulam*. He was cast opposite Rani Mukherjee, who had done just one film before this. The film met with lukewarm success at the box-office but the audience got to see Aamir in an unconventional role. Most of them came out from the theatres impressed by his performance. For the first time, Aamir lent his voice to a song in this film. He rehearsed the song till he got the tune right. What compelled him to do this? The character in the film could not be a trained singer, so using a regular playback was not a good idea. Experimenting with his untrained voice would be far more authentic. The reasoning worked. Soon the song '*Aati Kya Khandala*' was on the lips of music lovers. Maybe it was destined to be so. After all, Aamir once remarked in *The Free Press Journal*, 'I love singing as it puts me in a good mood. It disturbs the hell out of everyone around me, but it makes me feel very happy.' By this time, Aamir had made up his mind on having an ace up his sleeve with each upcoming film. He made himself scarce and doing lesser films was just a part of his strategy of moving up the ladder.

In the same year he did Deepa Mehta's *Earth*, which was adapted from Bapsi Sidhwa's famous book *Ice Candy Man* (also called *Cracking India*). He played Dil Navaz, a candy seller, in a story set before the Partition of India. His role in this film was a complete contrast to his image and the character of Siddharth in *Ghulam*. The Muslim character with kohl-lined eyes, sometimes depicting joy and otherwise full of anger, gave Aamir a sly, negative look. Aamir recalled that on seeing the film his sister called from New Jersey and cried a lot. She could not believe how her beloved brother could portray such a cold-blooded, villainous character so convincingly. His work was appreciated in both the films. He seemed to have struck a fine balance between commercial and parallel cinema. These films established him as a versatile actor. His policy seemed to be working in his favour. *Earth* was critically acclaimed and added

Sridevi, Aamir's favourite heroine, in a song from Roop Ki Rani Choron Ka Raja.

to his rich repository of work. At this time even though the producers were eager to sign him they were being turned away. They had to wait for their turn. The 'grandmaster' was now making the right moves, which made his contemporaries look up to him. His work ethics, well fleshed out characters and painstaking homework was giving positive results.

Working with directors having the correct vision has now become the actor's priority. He was comfortable signing and shooting with the current breed of visionaries. This included John Mathew Matthan, who had been an assistant director for several films and was in the world of advertising. He had waited long for the actor in order to cast him in his first film *Sarfarosh* in 1999. Though Aamir was impressed with the character of ACP Ajay Singh Rathod and liked the script, he was not sure of John's capability as a film director. He offered to buy the script but when John refused, he asked him to wait for his dates, only to study his work in that period. John created a fresh pair of Aamir and Sonali Bendre along with a formidable cast that included Naseeruddin Shah for this film. The film was on border terrorism and introduced a new shade of the actor. Even without the uniform, Aamir cut a smart figure as ACP Rathod. '*Sarfarosh* appealed to me because it was a mainstream film attempting to tackle the issue of Hindus and Muslims living together,' Aamir elaborated. In his own way, he said that he tried to counter the negativity that some people were spreading. Instead of fighting negativity, he tried to spread positivity through this film. The film had fabulous songs and a hint of patriotism; it was the hit of the year. When asked which of his films can have a sequel, Aamir proudly mentioned *Sarfarosh* and *Andaz Apna Apna*, as these were good films that had interesting endings.

As Aamir's credibility rose, so did his confidence. He created his niche while other actors still stuck to the old formulas that the industry followed. While other actors have exploited the star system of the industry, Aamir set an example for the new generation of actors to emulate.

Aamir never stuck to his hit pair with any actresses, including Juhi Chawla who was his close friend. 'Juhi is one of my closest friends. We spend hours in each other's make-up rooms. We don't care a damn about filthy minds,' Aamir said to *Filmfare* in 1995. He always maintained a good balance between his personal and professional life. He never hesitated to pair with new actresses like Raveena Tandon, Karisma Kapoor and Ayesha Jhulka. He was once asked which other heroines he wished to be paired with and he promptly replied, 'Sridevi!' He once mentioned that he wants Sridevi to be the heroine in all his films. 'I'm in love with her. I would love to do a *Summer of '42* with her. I wonder if I will ever get the chance,' he said in an interview to *Filmfare* in 1988. But the two of them were never starred together. It was only recently that Sridevi was seen on his television show *Satyamev Jayate*.

In the new millennium, Aamir's stock has grown threefold. As an actor he was moving from one achievement to another. He picked the right scripts and roles and with every film changed his image. Though reinvention has never been easy for anyone as it involves a number of risks, it comes very naturally to Aamir and he is proud of himself for attempting this in every film, 'If there's any actor who has taken the most number of risks, it's I. I have consistently done films which are completely against the tide. Most stars like to follow one image they know will work with the audience. I'm one of the few who has tried to and actually managed to break that myth. I've done films in which people see me as a character, not as Aamir. They think of me as Bhuvan (*Lagaan*), different from Aakash (*Dil Chahta Hai*) or Inspector Rathod from *Sarfarosh*.' His father would be happy to know that the success that eluded him, his son has received in great measure. *Lagaan* became another defining moment in his life. It was the making of another classic in the chronicles of the Indian film industry. It rightly deserves a huge mention in his growth as a producer-actor.

LAGAAN

PANGS OF A FIRST-TIME PRODUCER

> *I gave Ashutosh only one guideline: 'Don't compromise. Don't tell me later, "I wish I had got this". Whatever you want, you are going to get.'*

A scene from Lagaan *where the characters celebrate their victory in the cricket match.*

Facing page: Aamir at a Tata Sky press conference.

The international press thinks it's one of the best 25 sports movies of all time. The Oscars thought it was one of the best foreign language films of 2001. The world loves the story of the underdogs, and when you add cricket and romance to the mix, you have an all-rounder. Thus, when a peasant of Champaner, India challenges the British authorities to a game of cricket and agrees to pay three times the state tax (*lagaan*) if he loses the match, the entire world stands in his support. Yes,

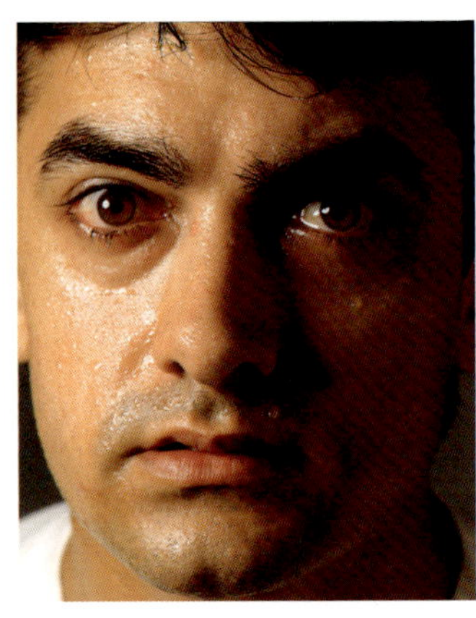

The intensity and passion on Aamir's face, so evident in his acting.

we are talking about *Lagaan*. Made with a modest budget of Rs 25 crore, it brought back the charm of rustic stories to Indian cinema. Audiences cheered more for Aamir Khan's character called Bhuvan, hitting a six on the final delivery than they did when M.S. Dhoni performed a similar feat at the World Cup. It wasn't just the entertainment; the film touched the aspirations of a billion Indians. It made us believe that we were truly empowered. That we could sing for the rains, that we could hope for miracles, because in hope lies our greatest strength.

Films like *Lagaan* come once in millennium. From the time it was grabbed in spirit (by the makers), it had the makings of a classic. However, the *Lagaan* spirit was not created overnight. It was created with the efforts and sacrifices of hundreds of people. The tremendous commitment and teamwork of the unit members showed in each frame. The spirit of *Lagaan* was such that Aamir decided to hold the first public screening of India's most awaited film at a modest theatre in the tiny city of Bhuj. A spirit that made the British cast travel over 5,000 miles to attend the show. And the spirit that made thousands of Kutchis overcome their personal tragedies (a massive earthquake had hit Gujarat in 2001, with its epicentre in Bhuj) to celebrate the release of their film. Aamir, who had adopted the entire village of Kunwaria where he had shot the film, became an unsung hero of hundreds of people he had helped in the time of that tragedy.

As much as the film was admired, so was the making of it. The journey of the making of *Lagaan* in itself is a remarkable story. Eventually it was a journey that was immortalised on celluloid. It is still spoken of in endearing terms as it has become an integral part of Indian cinematic history and Aamir can pat his back for supporting the risky project. Had Aamir Khan Productions not made this film how would the lovable character of Bhuvan be etched in film history? However, thinking big comes with a huge price tag, and the price that Aamir and his team had to pay is a case in point.

The prelude

Ashutosh Gowariker directed Lagaan, *which became a masterpiece in Indian film history.*

Ashutosh Gowariker was so obsessed with his story idea that he couldn't wait anymore to share it with Aamir, even if that meant narrating it to him in the wee hours of dawn. Ashutosh believed his story was so powerful that even a sleeping man would spring to life on hearing it but Aamir definitely felt otherwise. He found it outlandish and implausible and showed no interest. He told him, 'Look Ash, you've already made two films that haven't worked. This time around you must make something safe, something nice, not some weird story about villagers in British Raj.' But Ashutosh was determined not to give up.

His previous flops had forced him to ponder about what his aspirations were in life. Ashutosh realised the need to make something that he believed in and then hope that the audience too would like it and thus was born *Lagaan*. Even after Aamir's rejection, Ashutosh decided to develop his story idea into a full-fledged script and left Mumbai to write the dialogues version of *Lagaan* with Kumar Dave and Sanjay Dayma.

Once the script was complete, he requested Aamir for a meeting. After keeping Ashutosh on hold for a long time, Aamir finally agreed to listen to the script. He was shell-shocked after Ashutosh finished the narration. Aamir had experienced various emotions during the narration and was deeply moved by the script of *Lagaan*. 'How did you even conceive of such an idea Ash? It's simply superb...,' said Aamir. However, he knew well that the sensibility of this film made it an expensive experiment. The only way to make it work was to turn it into a mainstream film but he

Bhuvan (Aamir) with the two beautiful ladies, Gauri (Gracy Singh) and Elizabeth (Rachel Shelley), in Lagaan.

was not sure whether the audience would accept it. On Aamir's suggestion, Ashutosh tried but failed to convince any producer and actor to do this film on the credibility of its script. However, the script had Aamir intrigued. He wanted to share his experience with as many as possible. Aamir's creative ambition and love for challenge had made *Lagaan* irresistible. But he had to be crazy to do this film and crazy he was; Aamir decided to produce the film to maintain its integrity. In the life of the infant *Lagaan*, this was the turning point.

For the team's selection, Aamir's criteria were simple—anyone who would get involved with *Lagaan* should believe in its script and the director. As asked by Aamir, Ashutosh once again narrated the

Flashing his enigmatic smile.

story of *Lagaan*, but this time to film financier Jhamu Sughand and Aamir's close family members. This was the litmus test for the movie. Jhamu agreed to finance their ambitious venture and since then, he never looked back. Irrespective of how much the film overshot its budget, how great the delay happened in its release, how many times aesthetic and creative decisions overrode practical considerations, he backed the film without ever questioning Aamir.

Making this film was going to be an uphill task for Aamir, which only he could conquer, with loads of conviction and guts. But producing a film was like setting up a mammoth factory and he couldn't do that without the help of someone whom he could completely rely on. Though he knew that nothing in Reena's past had equipped her for the task of film production, she was the one Aamir wanted to share his responsibilities with so that he could focus on the creative side. Initially, Reena was not sure but she soon prepared herself with Aamir's assurance to teach and help her in times of need.

Numbers had also been Reena's strength and thus, Aamir wanted her to oversee the financial aspects of the project. For three months, Reena poured herself into the task along with Nikhat, Aamir's sister. Reena recalled, 'There were so many things happening at the same time, that I could not believe that it would all ever come together and a shot would ultimately be canned.' She soon discovered that the 8 crore budget prepared by Ashutosh was inadequate and *Lagaan* would require not less than 14 crore. Aamir's brief to his executive producer was clear, 'Reena, you must ensure that *Lagaan* does not exceed its budget and we are

*Sunil Alagh, ex-MD and CEO of Britannia, with Aamir and Ashutosh watching the cricket match between the two teams—*Lagaan *and Britannia, at Brabourne Stadium.*

not forced to put in endless amounts of money to complete the film. If that means you have to clamp down on me, please do so.'

Aamir with Reena at a film party.

Whether or not Reena needed *Lagaan*, no one can doubt that *Lagaan* needed Reena. 'I could not have made this film without Reena. I am not saying this as a husband. I mean I just *could not* have made this film without her,' said Aamir. Reena's involvement also had a strong romantic angle for Aamir. Now even professionally, they were building something together; exploring a new dimension of their relationship. There was growing mutual respect for new and different reasons.

Aamir had repeatedly seen how production goof-ups impacted the creative team in various ways; therefore he was determined not to let this happen under his production banner. But to achieve that, a properly organised and professional production department imbued with a modern work culture was required to be set up. Although, cast and crew juggling dates over several projects was an accepted work culture in the Indian film industry, Aamir knew that the same would be fatal for *Lagaan*. Thus the entire film must be shot from start to finish in a single schedule, during which every unit member will only live the world of *Lagaan*, decided Aamir. Whoever wished to be a part of the movie had to accept this work culture. He requested his childhood friend Satyajit Bhatkal to join them in achieving this. Nitin Desai, considered a part of his home team by Ashutosh, joined hands with him and started the search for locations with the director. He relished the challenge of making the audience smell the cow dung of Champaner through his sets. Anil Mehta, an old friend of Ashutosh and Aamir, excitedly joined them as the cinematographer. Javed Akhtar was the first choice to pen the songs for the movie but the lyricist after hearing the script, asked Aamir not to make this film as the script violated all sacred commandments of the market. But by then Aamir had made his decision. Years later, Aamir informed the audience in a TV show *Aap Ki Adalat* that though Javed sahab found his decision suicidal, he finally agreed to write the songs for them.

With Preity Zinta in the hummable song 'Jaane kyun' *from* Dil Chahta Hai *directed by Farhan Akhtar.*

When it came to music, they knew that A.R. Rahman was indispensable for their film. Though on Jhamu's request Rahman agreed to compose for the movie, Aamir wanted him to hear the script first. It was an unusual request from the producer for someone like Rahman, for whom producers stand in queue for several months. Usually impassive Rahman was pretty responsive to Ashutosh's script. But the challenge for Rahman was to compose all the songs two months before the shooting would start. Though Rahman agreed, his track record made Aamir nervous. He had no choice but to wait.

Whilst Rahman wrote the movie's main choral theme, Aamir sat outside the studio waiting for Rahman. After Aamir heard it, he went inside with moist eyes and said to Rahman, 'A.R., what a great feeling this is. My movie is made now!' Rahman reminisces to *Time* magazine, 'I saw a childlike honesty in Aamir's eyes.'

As costumes were important to create the period feel, they chose the first Indian Oscar-winning costume designer Bhanu Athaiya. To ease the work pressure of Reena and Nikhat, B. Shrinivas Rao joined as Chief Executive, Production. Aamir wanted someone who could ensure that the shooting would happen on schedule. When he enquired with his *Dil Chahta Hai* producer/director Farhan Akhtar to suggest someone, Apoorva Lakhia's name popped up. He had regularly worked as an assistant director (AD) on several projects in Hollywood. Aamir met Apoorva at 3 am in New York after a stage performance and Apoorva joined *Lagaan* as first AD.

To strike a balance between the conflicting pulls of authenticity and comprehensibility, poet K.P. Saxena was roped in to write the dialogues in Awadhi. The actors now had a new challenge to deal with—learning this language. They also decided to shoot *Lagaan* with sync sound though they knew well that the financial viability of the film depended highly on the adhering to the schedule and sync sound could prove to be disastrous to this. Aamir was in awe of the power of sync sound. He didn't want to compromise on that front and thus chose Nakul Kamte for this crucial job. Nakul had done a remarkable job of recording clean sound even at a crowded railway station in the film *Bhopal Express*, which had impressed Aamir and Ashutosh big time.

Lagaan *memorabilia: a bat containing signatures of all the players in the* Lagaan *cricket team.*

By now, Ashutosh also started looking around for actors. Gracy Singh bagged the role of Bhuvan's love interest after being auditioned with numerous other girls. Aamir and Ashutosh jointly selected her as her earthy looks and dancing skills suited the role. Other Indian actors for the supporting characters were

Satyajit Bhatkal directed a documentary on the making of Lagaan *and also wrote a book on it.*

also finalised after rigorous auditions. As a first-time producer, Aamir was being tossed from one part of the world to another. He had a nerve-racking time in England seeking English actors. The requirement was unique, he needed British actors who could speak Hindi and also play cricket. After facing a lot of difficulties, finally with the help of casting agent Danielle Roffe, they were able to put the British cast in place. On some occasions, Aamir was unhappy with the choices his production team had made. Some of the artists were finalised and then replaced, which irritated Reena and Ashutosh. But Aamir handled the situation tactfully by offering them infinite budgets to conduct fresh auditions.

Creating an entire village with people required the aid of the local people living there. Ashutosh had to do prompt auditions in Kutch, while the sets were being constructed! Nearly sixty actors to play members of the families were selected from Mumbai and Kutch. However, one of the biggest challenges was to create facilities for hundreds of people arriving from Mumbai and far away England. In Bhuj, far away from the location, Sahajanand Towers was refurbished to suit the metro crowd and their lifestyles. Near about sixty rooms were created, equipped with air conditioners, proper toilets and bedrooms.

The royal challenge

Shooting in the dry environs of Kutch, western Gujarat is by no means an easy job. The location does not support human habitation. To create a village existing in times of the British Raj became all the more daunting in such a place. Aamir Khan had just taken up the challenge to literally scale new heights, if not of Mount Everest, its equivalent. So when Shrinivas Rao from production faced difficulty in convincing a contractor, Danabhai Ahir to help construct the sets, Aamir invited him for a discussion over lunch at his home in Mumbai. Aamir explained to Danabhai how important the village of Champaner was to the film and how only he could create it. Danabhai's heart melted and he was convinced that working for Aamir Khan was going to be a life-changing experience for him. Once again, when no one was able to convince the Maharao of Kutch for allowing the team to use his palace for shooting, Aamir waved his magic wand. Like on the royal blood, his charm was equally effective on meagre farmers, whom he convinced to lease out their lands on which the village of Champaner and the cricket ground was made.

He was about to make a film that pooled in human resources from different cultures and races—with a single point of concentration—to make a complete entertainer. The royal challenge was taken with the help of only trusted aides, friends and a very talented team that handled production of an epic proportion for the very first time. Aamir's family had come in full support in the desert region of Kutch on the first day of the shoot. It was a moment in time, a new landmark in his career. It was the holy month of Ramzan and along with Aamir, there were other Muslim actors who were keeping *rozas* (fasting during the day) while at work. As a producer, Aamir conducted the pooja for the *mahurat* shot while he fasted!

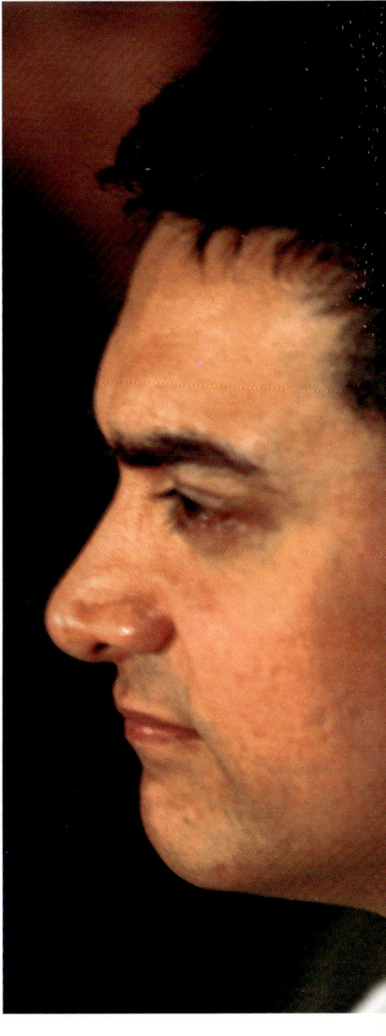

In a contemplative mood.

While Aamir was working towards establishing a different work culture, Apoorva was setting his own benchmark to achieve the targets Aamir had set for him. The schedule set was so tight that Apoorva needed to ensure everything worked like clockwork. He did so with the help of his assistants and a wonderful software—Movie Magic. Though it was a common tool used in Hollywood, it was first introduced in the Indian film industry with *Lagaan*. At Apoorva's command, every morning before the break of dawn the entire cast and crew had to assemble in the bus which would take them to the location. One day Aamir was late and the bus didn't wait for him. He had to reach the far flung location on his own. Even the lead actress Gracy Singh was left behind once to reach the location on her own on account of being late.

The team together faced several challenges and bravely overcame them during its filming. One of the oldest actors on set, A.K. Hangal

(Shambhukaka in the film) who died recently, had to be admitted to the hospital to nurse his back pain but despite his severe condition, resumed shoot to complete his scenes. He said, 'If I were to have left the film and gone back to Mumbai, what would have happened to the film? I decided, come what may, I'll shoot. I'll die with my boots on.' One fine day, Ashutosh accidentally developed severe back pain, confirmed as a case of slipped disc by the doctor. He was advised complete bed rest for at least three weeks. It is fascinating to note that the director conducted the shoot in that phase by bandaging himself to a portable bed.

The other incident that many '*Lagaanites*' would not forget was the bursting of the two large septic tanks. The two tanks were for the number of new toilets that were constructed on the sets. One fine day, while shooting the water from the septic tanks started leaking. It was a ticking bomb that was going to explode any minute. The assistants had to sort the problem immediately so that the shooting was not disturbed.

A British actress Katkin was so impressed by the 'Indianness' she experienced during the filming of *Lagaan*, she had her marriage arranged in the Champaner village temple that was created for

Interacting with the media at a press conference held in Film City, Mumbai.

the movie. She said, 'I believe in only one God, by whatever name you call it, and that God was there in that temple!' Reena and Aamir did her *kanyadaan*. Many other actors remember their time on the sets with nostalgia as each one looks back in gratitude for being a part of this slice of film history.

Aamir speaking at a press meet where the logo of his production house serves as a backdrop.

However, the film's making took its toll on almost the entire crew when the schedule was extended. By the end of the pre-decided shooting period the cast, crew and production team were barely in spirits. Everyone wanted to return home as soon as possible. Aamir donning the mantle of a producer, used his skills to convince each one to stay back to fulfil the dream they were now an integral part of. Everyone complied, though some of the team members had to reshuffle their personal and professional commitments to complete the shooting.

Aamir returned to Mumbai after shooting the talkies portion where another test was awaiting him. Along with the editor Ballu Saluja, Aamir had to struggle a lot to cut down the length of the film but still the final cut was lengthier than most Hindi movies. Despite warnings from industry experts, he decided to release one of the longest films ever made in India—all of three hours and forty-two minutes!

The magic of an unseen bond of love

Long after the crew had returned, news came that a huge earthquake had struck Bhuj. The crew had made friends with the families there on their first-ever outdoor as a production. When the production team and producers heard about the earthquake in the region they were heartbroken. Aamir returned to Bhuj and was extremely sad to learn about the disaster stories of destruction and death. Some of the villagers who were a part of the film's team had become homeless. Months later when Aamir and the team members returned with the edited film, they were yet again embraced by the villagers as family. A stronger bond had been made. Aamir, who was grateful to the villagers for arranging their stay in the summer months, made preparations to help out the villagers in their time of distress.

Sky is the limit

Aamir had high ambitions for the movie. He had made the film keeping the global audience in mind. This helped its selection in the Best Foreign Language Film category for the Oscars. It took another exciting learning curve when as a producer Aamir learnt how to exercise his skills to promote the film. He aggressively promoted it to guarantee that the jury members were aware of the project. It was his way of saying that the world's largest film producing country was capable of making a movie with high production values and a strong script. The film had no special effects, or complex editing. But it had a story of universal human value.

The film entered the syllabus of IIM, Indore as a case study. Many companies conducted workshops to learn how to handle human

Aamir at the release function of Bachchanalia, *a book on Amitabh Bachchan, in NCPA, Mumbai.*

A beautiful painting of Aamir and his team from Lagaan *by artist Partho Chatterjee.*

resources and get inspired by the team-building exercises under grace and pressure. Today *Lagaan* is a success story on and off the screen. Aamir's first director Ketan Mehta commented after watching the movie, 'I just saw *Lagaan* and I think Aamir has seasoned as an actor and I'd say he has balls of steel as a producer. I think it's a very courageous venture to invest so much of himself in—not in terms of money, but I'm sure it required a certain grave decision and I'm glad it was a courageous decision rather than a market driven tame decision.' Amitabh Bachchan exclaimed, 'The film is a piece of perfection—it's completely flawless—I've seen it a number of times already and not because I've done the voice over but because I've enjoyed it so much.'

Everyone associated with Aamir Khan Productions was proud to have been a part of this legacy. As for Aamir himself, it was just another milestone in his exciting life as an entertainer. He has stood the test of time. He has enlarged his vision furthermore. He has become a well-loved producer who would now only make and support films he would believe in under his banner. This was not the end; the star's priceless brand had gained more value.

AAMIR KHAN

by Rauf Ahmed

He is a law unto himself—somebody had once told me about Aamir Khan. He is very stubborn.

I thought that was unique about him. What people in the industry are cribbing about is 'his individuality' that sets him apart.

Aamir has had a clear take on it. 'You can't live to please a crowd. If you try you will have no individuality left.' He believes that an individual, however gregarious, is left to himself in the end, exposed to the consequences of his actions.

A great philosophy, they said, but will not make sense in the context of our film industry. However, to Aamir's credit, he has lived by his beliefs with uncanny determination. That's what has taken him where he is today, beyond the hundred and two hundred crore clubs.

For long, industry wags kept taking potshots at his 'rigid' points of view and 'weird' ways. They accused him of being a tiresome nitpicker whose 'interference' drove directors to the end of their tethers. Nevertheless, in the end, almost a decade and a half down the line, they found it impossible to ignore the difference his work has made. They can't argue anymore against results that are almost unimpeachable.

It's not easy to slot Aamir Khan. He has upstaged stereotypes. It's even more difficult put the Aamir Khan phenomenon in perspective in an industry sustained largely by a gambling instinct.

In a sombre frame of mind.

When two stalwarts from the industry, Anand Mahindra and Kumar Mangalam Birla, asked Aamir at an intellectual conclave organised by a leading news magazine, how he could pull off the seemingly impossible feat of blending art with commerce so consistently in a business largely driven by speculation, his answer was simple: 'I make films that I would like watching myself.' It was more than a simplistic quip. It suggested a vision which most mainstream filmmakers don't believe in.

The fact that Aamir's vision has time and again stormed the box-office is a stunning revelation that even mainstream flicks can have a mind, contrary to the perception. That a film like *Peepli (Live)* could command an initial draw comparable to a 'big' film was a measure of the credibility enjoyed by brand Aamir Khan. It's doubtful if the same film could have worked the same magic without his participation and presence!

Anand Mahindra with Aamir Khan at the launch of the Mahindra Mojo and Stallio motorcycles in India.

Facing page: In a scene from the soulful song 'Pehla Nasha' *in* Jo Jeeta Wohi Sikandar.

The process of building a credible brand had begun casually but backed by a smartly thought-out strategy. The manifestation began with *Ghulam* in 1998...

Aamir Hussain Khan's tryst with cinema had a rather inconspicuous beginning as an assistant to his paternal uncle Nasir Hussain, a wizard of romantic musicals in his heydays in the 1950s and the 1960s, which lasted for three years. With his height, as he once joked, he had 'no tall aspirations to become an actor'. ('I didn't think I had it in me to be an actor.') Acting happened by the way, when, in the mid-1980s, Ketan Mehta cast him opposite Kitu Gidwani in a small role in his film *Holi*. It was followed by *Raakh,* an experimental film directed by his close pal Aditya Bhattacharya. The film revealed glimpses of the class Aamir could achieve as an actor. He was just brilliant!

The performance won him an unexpected award—a National Award in 1989, specially recommended by the jury! The young protagonist of *Raakh*, Aamir explained, 'was a naive, impulsive boy who came from a background similar to mine, and Aditya wanted me to put as much of myself into it as possible.' The hero was named 'Amir Hussein' as well. 'But the behaviour and actions of the hero were fictional,' he clarified.

Aamir's first release *Qayamat Se Qayamat Tak* (*QSQT*) directed by his first-cousin Mansoor Khan (son of Nasir Hussain) not only revived the 'romantic musical' as a genre, but gave to the industry a fresh young star of exceptional potential. The film had come at a time when the Amitabh Bachchan era had outlived itself and the film industry was groping for a new formula to replace the violence and gore routine that had held sway for over a decade.

After a sluggish opening week, *QSQT* had gained momentum to become a huge hit! Aamir's stock went soaring with blockbusters like *Dil*, *Jo Jeeta Wohi Sikandar* and *Dil Hai Ke Manta Nahin* following his debut. Overnight, Aamir was hot property. The euphoria also opened up the usual pitfalls, the most dangerous one being the rush of producers to sign on the 'new superstar'.

In his hurry to explore his own range as an actor, as Aamir admitted candidly, he did sign a few nondescript films which inevitably began raising questions about his staying power as a star. Like it invariably happens when a rising star falters, the media got after him, the tirade soon turning to his personal life. It did drive him into a shell, which was rather unfortunate as he was the most articulate among his contemporaries. However, to Aamir's credit, instead of retaliating, he chose to take the attack in his stride and quietly went about reinventing himself and recasting his career moves.

He reflected: 'Why did I do those films? I kept asking myself. For quick bucks? I had enough money to lead a comfortable life. And I am not the kind who

Keenly observing the proceedings during the video launch of the first song of Dhoom: 3.

relishes exhibitionism.' He used to drive around in a modest car. It was a Maruti Esteem at one stage, if I remember right. His wife at that time, Reena would travel from Bandra to her place of work in South Bombay by local trains. 'These things are not important,' he said dismissively. 'I need a decent enough car to move around.' For years he lived in a modest flat as well. Things might have changed over the years, but not the man. His convictions have continued to sustain themselves.

In the early 1990s, Aamir took a break to reorient his approach to work. When he resumed, his involvement in the process of making a film had become deeper and more serious. He co-scripted *Hum Hain Rahi Pyar Ke* with Mahesh Bhatt. The film was a huge hit. The intensity continued with every film that followed. He became 'more meticulous about the choice of scripts and directors'. He also became more particular about work ethics. Some of the veterans in the industry derided his plain-speaking manner and the tendency to ask questions a 'holier-than-thou' attitude.

During the making of *Ghulam*, Aamir strongly objected to a totally detached Mahesh Bhatt retiring to a corner of the set with a novel and asking his nephew Vikram Bhatt to direct the film. After the first few days, Aamir walked up to Mahesh and said, 'If Vikram is going to direct the film, you should withdraw your name and designate him as director.' A stunned Mahesh retorted, 'That's for me to decide, I am the producer of the film.'Aamir was equally defiant. 'But it's not acceptable to me,' he said. 'You can't take credit for a film directed by someone else. If you have a problem designating Vikram, who is actually doing the job as the director, I'll walk out of the film.' Mahesh was livid. 'How can you quit the film at this stage? Who will pay for scrapping the portions already shot with you?' he countered. 'I will. Send me a bill, you'll get a cheque,' said Aamir without batting an eyelid and walked away. An upset Mahesh had a quick meeting with his brother and partner Mukesh Bhatt and decided to take a sensible way out. He stepped down and let Vikram Bhatt take over as the director of *Ghulam*.

When Mahesh Bhatt went to the press accusing Aamir of 'playing God', Aamir's reply was: 'I hold Mr Mahesh Bhatt in high esteem. I had enjoyed working with him in films like *Dil Hai Ke Manta Nahin* and *Hum Hain Rahi*

Pyar Ke, but I couldn't believe it when I saw a director of his standing sitting and reading a novel on the set of a film he had signed me for and asking his assistant to direct. It was one of the saddest and most traumatic moments of my life when I had to turn around and point out to him that he was not doing his job. I won't accept any director signing me for a film and asking his assistant to direct me. I have no problem working with Vikram. I would have happily worked with him had he been officially designated director.'

A few people from the industry did fault Aamir's 'rigid' stand on the facile plea of 'seniority' and 'gratitude' (Mahesh had been very supportive of Aamir in the early stage of his career), but nobody could find fault in him professionally. But then, professionalism is not among the virtues applauded by many in the film industry.

Aamir had developed great rapport with Vikram Bhatt during the making of *Hum Hain Rahi Pyar Ke*, where he initially had been Mahesh Bhatt's assistant. Vikram grabbed the opportunity and reworked on the screenplay of *Ghulam* and made it slicker. He also replaced a reluctant Pooja Bhatt with Rani Mukherjee. The cult number '*Aati kya Khandala*' which gave *Ghulam* a huge boost at the box-office, was a brainchild of the Aamir-Vikram combo. The film turned out to be one of the biggest hits of 1998.

I remember meeting Aamir on the eve of the release of *Sarfarosh* directed by a first-time director, John Mathew Matthan. He was very tense. Was it the speculation around the sensitive subject of the film that was bothering him? Or was he apprehensive of the press waiting to pounce on him if the film were to backfire at the box-office? His grim look turned to a smile. 'No,' he denied, 'neither of it. I turn a fatalist before the release of every film of mine. In the state I'm in right now, if someone were to tell me that this building is on fire, I might just say ok and stay put...'

Planning his next move in the movie Sarfarosh.

Facing page: Naseeruddin Shah as Gulfam Hassan and Aamir as ACP Rathod in a scene from Sarfarosh.

Lost in his thoughts at a special photo shoot for Mann.

About the curiosity and speculations around the film, he said, 'I think it's natural. The film dwells on a serious subject. It's about terrorism, but it confines itself to how terrorism affects innocent human lives ... It's not a didactic film.' *Sarfarosh* turned out be a huge hit achieving what Aamir had dreamt of—a sensible film that reaches out to the largest possible audience.

Karan (extreme left), Daljeet 'DJ', Flt Lt Ajay, Sonia, Aslam and Sukhi from Rang De Basanti.

I have known John Mathew, who directed the film, for long. During the making of the film I had asked him about Aamir's much-maligned predilection to interfere in the director's work. 'I think that's a canard,' said John. 'To have an actor like him in my film was like having another mind. His concern is never about his role or his performance. It's always about the film. I found his involvement a great asset.'

Much later, when Aamir agreed to do *Rang De Basanti*, Rakeysh Omprakash Mehra was pleasantly surprised. He had been sceptical about Aamir joining a group of young actors as one among them. So, when he said 'yes', he thought he should make his role more substantial to match his star status. But Aamir stunned him by stopping him. 'Please don't tamper with the script or my role,' he said. 'It is for me to fit into the role, I don't want you to tailor it for me. I like the script as it is.' Mehra couldn't believe his ears.

Aamir in a rain dance with Kareena Kapoor in the song 'Zoobi Doobi' *from* 3 Idiots.

Contradicting the general perception that he was irritatingly finicky and methodical in his approach to life and work, Aamir had once said, 'I do set a standard and go all out to achieve it. I don't think that's a negative trait. Methodical? Maybe I am, to some extent. It seems to have come from my early interest in chess. But I don't think I'm all that methodical. Nor am I very calculative. Most of the crucial decisions in my life had been impulsive ... like my decision to quit studies, my (first) marriage, my decision to become an actor have all been impulsive, split-second decisions.'

'He is just mad!' a friend had joked about him once. But there certainly is a method in his madness. He has barely made a false move after that initial clumsy spell in his career. Interestingly, he chose to kick-start the 'new phase' in his career in association with an erratic genius, Ram Gopal Varma. A path-breaking film, *Rangeela* showcased a tougher Aamir Khan. The transition

Aamir with the entire cast and crew of Peepli (Live).

from the 'cute' romantic to the macho lover was complete with *Ghulam*. The range has been extending.

From *Rangeela* onwards, brand Aamir has remained a formidable force at the box-office. It could sell a *Delhi Belly* and *Peepli (Live)* as effectively as a *Ghajni* and a *3 Idiots*. An occasional adventure like *Mangal Pandey: The Rising* might have come unstuck but it wasn't a shot in the dark. Even his run as a producer, which began with the cult film *Lagaan* has been just spectacular—a remarkable testimony to his extraordinary grasp over a medium which has forever been considered unpredictable. He has pulled off difficult ventures with young directors without looking at their track record. He worked with Ashutosh Gowariker on *Lagaan* ignoring the earlier two flops against his name.

'Hits and flops,' he believes, 'are no reflection of a director's merit. At best they might reflect his business sense. You need talent to deliver quality.'

Talent and that inexplicable spark within, which lights unknown terrains, have been leading him on ... from one milestone to another.

Rauf Ahmed has been the former editor of Super, Movie, Filmfare *and* Screen.

the actor prepares

'I don't emulate anyone. I just follow my own path.'

Aamir never makes any effort to set trends. But unknowingly ends up becoming a trendsetter. He puts in a lot of thought in finding the best possible routes to accomplish important tasks. Much to everyone's surprise, his instinct usually turns out to be right, no matter how bizarre the chosen course is. Quite effortlessly he has established several examples of his unique approach to various characters he has played and the methods he has used to prepare himself for these roles.

At the beginning of his career, as an actor, he did not put much thought about the characters he portrayed on the silver screen. He wasn't even formally trained in acting. But a sharp photographic mind boosted his chances of following a career in acting successfully. 'When I read a script, it just goes straight to my brain. It's like a computer in its memory. It just soaks everything in and then it's in my head at all times where it gets processed,' says Aamir. He still remembers the lines that he had to say as a painter in his first-ever play in Gujarati in Class 12, a role which he couldn't actually perform as he was sacked for missing a day's rehearsal. The lines remain etched in his 'hard drive'.

Applying a finishing touch to his look before a shot.

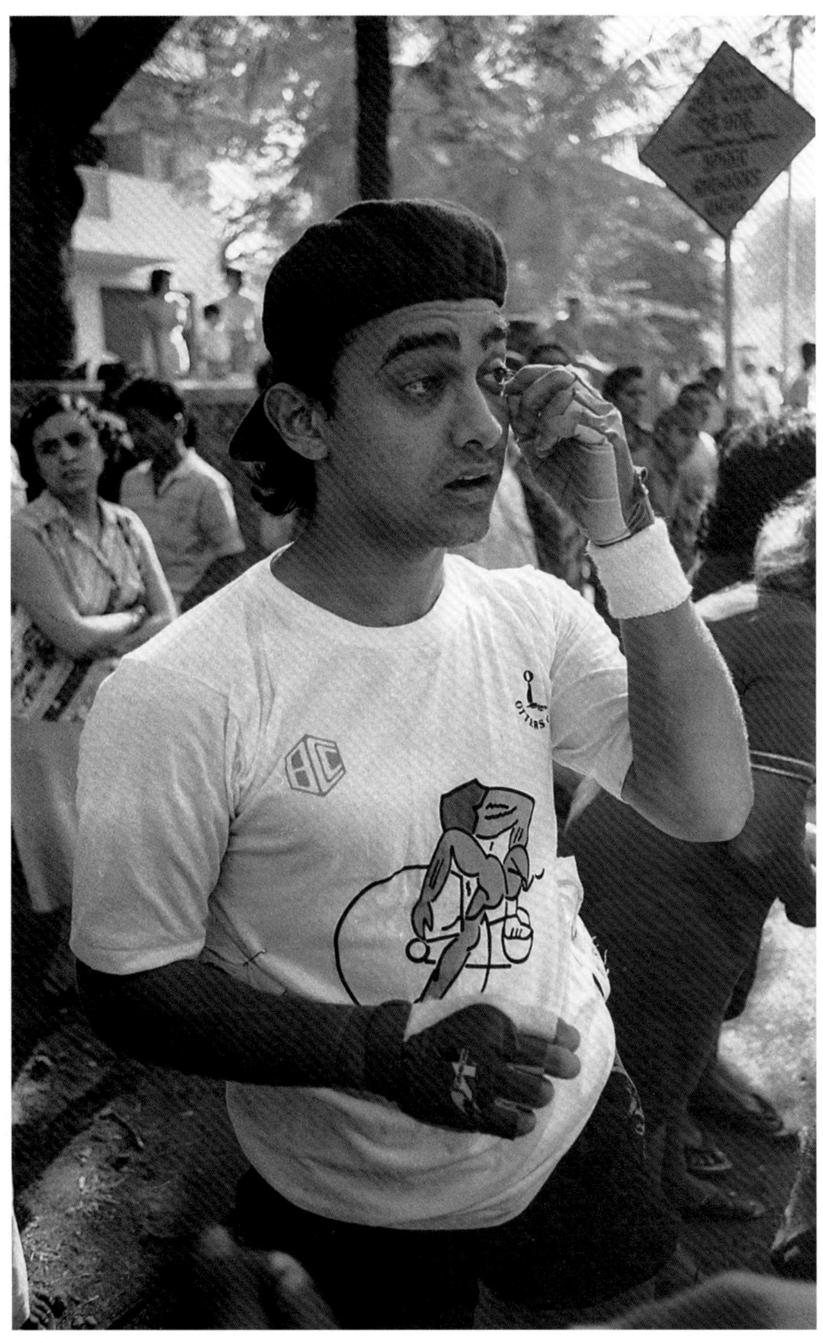

In his early years, Aamir Khan did not do anything noticeable to create a fashion craze amongst his fans. Though Aamir had an enormous fan following post his debut movie, it did not set any style statement. Like the film *Bobby* (starring Rishi Kapoor and Dimple Kapadia) that brought large sunglasses, short polka-dotted skirts, flared trousers and bell-bottoms to the fore, *QSQT* remained quite nondescript in the fashion department. However, when Salman Khan's debut movie *Maine Pyar Kiya* hit the theatres, the market was flooded with friendship caps and costumes similar to the ones the leading lady Bhagyashree wore in the film. Even the dialogues like '*Dosti ka ek oosul hai* madam ... no sorry, no thank you' [Friendship has one rule madam ... no sorry, no thank you] and '*Dosti ki hai, nibhani toh padegi*' [If you have committed to be friends, you must fulfil its duties too] clicked instantly with the younger crowd.

Preparing for a cycle race from Juhu to Bandra to promote Jo Jeeta Wohi Sikandar.

Facing page: A side profile of Aamir during a photo shoot at 1 am for Mangal Pandey.

In the second phase of his acting career, he started working towards building his personality to suit the characters he played. In the process, he introduced some fashion fads, hairstyles, fitness mantras and mannerisms that were highly discussed by the media and widely adopted by his fans. Within the industry, he has introduced new levels of professionalism, a sense of discipline, commitment to prepare oneself for a character through various techniques and sourcing better formats to work.

For Vikram Bhatt's *Ghulam*, Aamir took time to work on the character. The entire 'look' was devised to suit the role. The work behind the scenes became very apparent on the screen like the tight T-shirts, different kinds of rings on his fingers, colourful vests, leather jackets and the chains round his neck. He had added many important accessories to the get-up of the 'bad boy' and it worked wonders to create the image needed to convince the audience about his character. After *Ghulam*'s release, many youngsters were seen on two-wheelers, riding past the sunset vrooming on the mean streets. While deciding the look, Aamir had only considered the character and not whether the 'look' would start a trend amongst the cinegoers.

To lend more credence to the character of Siddharth in *Ghulam*, Aamir attempted playback singing for the first time with the song '*Aati Kya Khandala?*' (a duet with singer Alka Yagnik). Aamir practised and worked hard to get the notes right. It took many days of rehearsals before he stood in front of the mike to record the song. His efforts paid off and on its release, the song became an instant hit among all especially young men trying to woo their girlfriends.

Left: John Mathew Matthan, the director of Sarfarosh; *Right: Dressed as a woman in* Baazi.

Facing page: For the promotion of Sarfarosh, *Aamir agreed to pose for a statue by standing 4 to 5 hours at a sculptor's studio in Goregaon.*

For the promotion of *Sarfarosh*, Atmanand of Studio Link, who worked on several films of Aamir, suggested to get a statue of Aamir made for the film's promotion. But when the sculptor refused to refer a photograph for creating the statue and demanded Aamir to be present in person, director John Mathew lost all hope. Due to this clause, he was even apprehensive to mention the idea to Aamir. No one ever imagined that an actor of such a stature would ever agree to stand still for four to five hours to get a statue made. But Aamir understood the need of the moment and complied!

To say that Aamir has learnt about his craft is not sufficient. He has been able to put meaning into every performance. For instance, when he shot for *Baazi*, he was required to wear a woman's costume for a dance sequence. He actually went through the routine of waxing his legs. He could have had it easier by shaving the hair but he wanted to know what women go through when they waxed their hair. This hair-raising experience made the actor understand what it is to dress like a woman. Would he do it again? Not if given the choice, but he had to undergo the metamorphosis for the song sequence '*Dole dole dil dole*'.

Aamir has always thought deeply about his characters, so be it Bhuvan's stance in *Lagaan*, with his chest out and his weight evenly distributed on his legs to suggest inner strength, or the emotional yet naughty eyes of Akash in *Dil Chahta Hai*, he has always been precise with the attitude required to convince the audience that what they are watching on screen is not Aamir Khan but the character he portrays in those films. Now no one would argue with the observation that film scholar Nasreen Munni Kabir once made, 'Khan thinks in close-up, wide shot and mid-shot, in total physicality.' While filming for *Lagaan*, he learnt Awadhi from an actor-writer Raja Awasthi and moulded himself into a villager. With the same ease, he transformed himself to an uber-cool man in *Dil Chahta Hai* that released in the same year as *Lagaan*. He sported a new hairstyle with a soul patch (a small beard under the lower lip and above the chin). His classy executive suits, blazers and ties became a rage among the younger generation.

Despite being a teetotaller, he drank almost a full bottle of vodka in order to lend reality to the character of a drunken man for a scene in *Raja Hindustani*. He felt extremely uncomfortable after every peg but still continued drinking until they canned the scene. He did dangerous stunts like jumping in front of a running train, risking his life, to execute a scene in *Ghulam*. He changed his physical appearance and grew his hair and moustache to suit the role of Mangal Pandey, which took him more than a year. He not only endures pains to get into the skin of the characters but is also famous for manipulating people and situations to give the perfect shot. For instance, to get a well-tanned look during the shooting of *Mangal Pandey: The Rising*, he would randomly invite crew members and co-stars to play chess with him. Sitting under the blazing sun, one of the actors Murli Sharma once wondered as to why Aamir was so keen of playing chess under such high temperatures. He used to comply with Aamir until he discovered this was his means of getting tanned and ready for the role before the shot was to be taken.

Working on wardrobe, styling, hair and looking the part were just few of the exciting things he has done to get into the skin of the characters. Seeing Aamir work hard on the role before the shoot prompted many other actors to make their roles more credible by styling themselves and creating a wardrobe. However, by then Aamir had moved on further to give integrity to his screen looks. Some examples of his complete makeovers can be seen in films like *Ghajini* and *3 Idiots*.

For *Ghajini*, he underwent a remarkable alteration in his real-life persona to portray the character. Even in his forties, his passion for work had not dimmed. His eight-pack abs and peculiar haircut produced a menacing appearance of a business tycoon turned avenger. It showed he had become tough and underwent rigorous training to achieve it. On watching the Tamil version of the film he knew that mere training in the gym would not be enough. Thus, along with it, he appointed a dietician Dr Vinod A. Dhurandhar who monitored his diet closely. The director of the film A.R. Murugadoss had already visualised the character and he needed a well-toned guise. He wanted the rich, smartly attired Sanjay Singhania to attain a lean, mean form, full of vengeance. When the film was offered to Aamir, he was in the middle of directing *Taare Zameen Par*. He sought out a gym trainer Satyajit Chourasia (Satya) to train him to acquire the right look. The requirement of the role made the actor come up with a new strategy. He had to shift from the role of a simple drawing teacher in *Taare Zameen Par* to that of a businessman who had lost the love of his life and was seeking revenge in *Ghajini*. Arnold Schwarzenegger became the reference point for him. In 2009, when Aamir was asked to speak on how he built his body he explained, 'My trainer, Satyajit Chourasia, has a very intuitive mind and a good understanding of the mind and body of the person he is training. That is very important. Once you choose a good trainer, you must trust him completely. They are the experts and know better than us how our body responds to stress.'

Facing page: Aamir checking his hair and make-up on the sets of Isi Ka Naam Zindagi.

Aamir in an uber-cool look from Dil Chahta Hai.

His trainer was amazed at the way his client showed discipline. He expected 100 per cent effort but received much more involvement. The actor required pumping iron for three hours every single day, for nearly thirteen months. The garage at Marina Apartments, where Aamir lived, was transformed into a makeshift gym. Satya had already trained other actors like Hrithik Roshan, Zayed Khan, Rani Mukherjee, Esha Deol, Saif Ali Khan and Ajay Devgn in the past. From being 80 kilograms, Aamir lost 12 kilograms and got the eight-pack abs. When the posters of the film released, between the two, Aamir said, 'We could have done a lot better if I hadn't been slightly lax because of *Taare Zameen Par*.' He may not be satisfied with his efforts but his fans could not ask for more.

But why did he have to undergo this gruelling transformation? Aamir explained in his interview, 'I needed this kind of physique because the kind of action you see me doing, you will believe I am capable of only because of my body.' He added, 'It took three hours of workout every day. I began on March 15, 2007, one day after my birthday, and it went on till April 21, 2008,' he said. 'I learned a lot about fitness in this period. And how far I could push myself.' Revealing a little more he said, 'The workout was a cycle of three days. Mondays I did chest and back, Tuesdays I worked on the arms, and Wednesdays I exercised my shoulders and legs. Then I would repeat the cycle. This included cardio every day of between half an hour to an hour. And abs, to work the core muscles and get the six-pack, say 1,000 crunches. On days when I felt good, I would push myself more. There was no time to think … because I'd be screaming in pain! But I was particular about getting eight hours of sleep. No matter what time I went to bed, I'd get eight hours, then get up and start training. It was tough, because I was into post production for *Taare Zameen Par*. And I'd finish my workouts, shower, crash out for a while to regain strength, then go to work.'

It is remarkable to notice that only very few actors have ever before taken so many pains to fit themselves into a role. However, this is not just one example, there are many more.

Though Aamir's looks always won him an immense female fan base, with time, like other actors, he has also aged but that has never reflected on screen. Even today, he looks much younger than his fellow actors and credits his parents for his youthful looks saying, 'I guess it's in my genes.' Nevertheless, in the last five years, the actor has become extremely cautious of his diet. 'I have discovered that you are what you eat. So I am very particular about my diet, workout and sleep,' he informed. He takes a balanced diet. 'I have six small meals a day and my food is accurately measured. So I know how many calories I am consuming,' he stated. Unlike earlier years, he is now very particular about his workouts and unfailingly sleeps for eight hours. He also drinks about four litres of water every day. 'I maintain a very positive and balanced life. That's my secret,' Aamir revealed.

Whatever the character demands, the actor is always willing to do. For *3 Idiots*, when Aamir was required to undergo the reverse process of what he followed for *Ghajini*, he showed no qualms. To fit into this new role, he needed to look younger, like a college-going guy. Unlike the 1970s, when it was possible for even fifty-year-old actors to play college going character, today to look the part is vital. Though it was difficult to present a forty-plus actor as a college student to the audience, Aamir succeeded to look at least twenty years younger in *3 Idiots*. But how did he achieve that? He did so by changing his fitness regime and diet to match the other younger heroes in the film. His dietician planned a careful diet. He also started playing badminton, sometimes for even two hours a day, with students at IIM, Bangalore where the film was shot for over a month. He had to let go of the eight packs; his painfully acquired lean look for *Ghajini*. But his efforts again paid off and the film was a smash hit.

Aamir takes complete interest in the project once he is committed to it, and *3 Idiots* is a great example of this. The film was promoted with a clear-cut

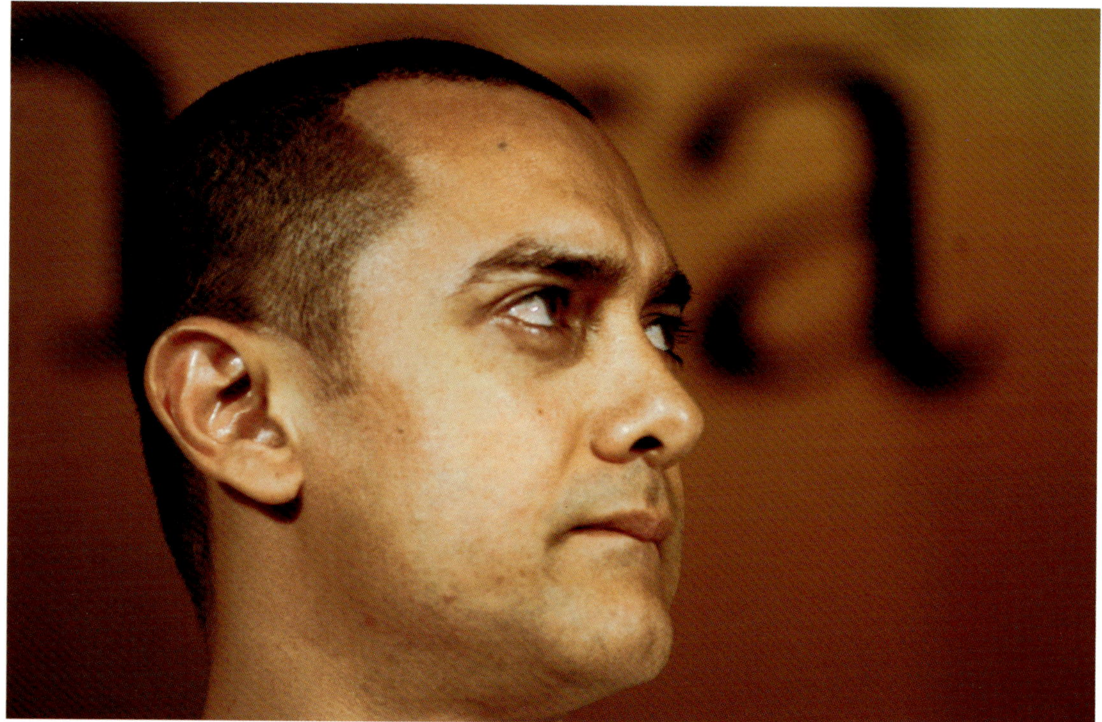

Right: A film still from Talaash *with Rani Mukherjee and Jineet Rath, the child artiste.*

Extreme right: Aamir and Karisma Kapoor looking glamorous in a shot from Raja Hindustani.

Facing page: At a press meet in his Ghajini *look.*

marketing strategy formulated by the star. It managed to beat all records at the box-office. At this time the star's willpower was also on the rise. He had quit smoking. He used to puff away more than forty cigarettes a day. But his family, especially his children, pushed him hard to leave this habit. Aamir said, 'The human mind is a very powerful tool. I realised this with the three-hours-a-day, six-days-a-week training I did for *Ghajini* for over a year. If it wants something badly, the body will give it. It's like what yogis say.' This could be one of the reasons he remains fresh all the time.

Aamir worked with another trainer, Dheepesh Bhatt, to prepare for his role as a cop in *Talaash*. When the trainer was interviewed by *Stardust* magazine in August 2012 for their issue of *Style* he said, 'The star did not miss any training sessions. I know now why he is called Mr Perfect. He gave me immense respect and I would like to train him again.' While *3 Idiots* required him to look younger and lose the eight-pack abs, in *Talaash* he had to learn swimming since the film had a couple of crucial underwater sequences. The actor who did not know how to swim, took swimming lessons to perfect those sequences. Within three months, he became an accomplished swimmer. The actor informed, 'My mom was always scared that something would happen to us in the water, so she never allowed my siblings or me to get into the pool. As a result, none of us learnt swimming. Thanks to *Talaash*, I got to learn one more thing.' Aamir also trained to get his basic hand and feet movements correct and learnt breathing techniques, which helped him stay underwater for long spans of time.

Aamir and Katrina Kaif interacting with the media at the merchandise launch of Dhoom: 3.

Facing page: Aamir and Reena interacting with Shekhar Kapur and his wife Suchitra Krishnamoorthi at Taj Hotel.

Ever since Yash Raj Films' announcement, one of the most anticipated films of Aamir, supposed to release in December 2013, has been *Dhoom: 3*. Aamir's interest to get into the training mode shows he is always ready to try new ways of remaining fit. He is learning acrobatics, the French technique of parkour and ballet for this film. He got a fitness trainer called David from America to help him achieve the perfect look for this film. Aamir is playing a gymnast and the antagonist in the film. Such was the significance of this transformation that the film's shooting dates were postponed so that he and his co-star Katrina could prepare for their action roles. Apart from rigorous training for action scenes, Katrina had to learn paragliding and singing. Soon we will see Aamir as a handsome baddie in this franchise.

Dr Deepak Chaturvedi, President, INDOMEDICON always quotes Aamir as a good example to all his patients when he talks about anti-aging. He believes

that anti-aging has lot to do with 'hormones' and 'lifestyle'. Thus, he is sure that Aamir's discipline in work is a reflection of his healthy lifestyle. 'As far as hormones are concerned, he has given an immense reflection of his high testosterone in flicks like *Sarfarosh* and *Ghajini*. The beauty of estrogen is visible in his charming personality in *3 Idiots*. His high adrenaline and thyroid activities are always visible in all his work. The best thing he does is that with his charm he makes oxytocin release in his viewers, which makes a bond between him and them. I can really see all hormones working high in Aamir and I hope that he continues to be in high spirits,' he stated. Like many others, director Shekhar Kapur also thinks that Aamir Khan has not aged since years. Aamir had been his first choice for his ambitious project *Time Machine* and though the film did not materialise, he is all praise for him, 'My first choice is Aamir because he has this vulnerable lost-in-space look. He is the kind of face that is timeless. It could belong to the forties and to the future. It has an ageless charm; untouched by cynicism that one sees etched on every face around us these days. I think Aamir is capable of recreating Dev Anand's suavity. His enthusiasm is reminiscent of a puppy eager to explore and experience every facet of his environment.'

Besides being genuine to his characters and committed to his work, Aamir has also been quite vocal about his thoughts regarding the changes he wishes to bring into the industry. 'Instead of five big stars, we should have twenty. We have to encourage young talent.' Along with many others, there are two most important changes that he would like to bring into the industry and has been advocating for them from a long time. He emphasised, 'The two changes in the industry I would want to see are; the profit-sharing system on a week-to-week basis should be done away with. Secondly, we need to value writers and pay them more.' To an extent he has been able to achieve this through his films but would like to take this forward in a big way. As an entertainer, he goes out of his way to breathe life into the roles. Every new film is a proof of his dedication to his craft.

IN HIS OWN TUNE

by Narendra Kusnur

Aamir has had an amazing musical innings ever since Qayamat Se Qayamat Tak *was released*

A quarter century later, that image still lingers. Clad in a sleeveless jacket over a white shirt, his tie hanging loose, his fingers strumming a guitar to the tune that went '*Papa kehte hain bada naam karega, beta hamara aisa kaam karega...*' Aamir Khan had hit the jackpot.

Though he had acted before in *Holi*, the 1988 film *Qayamat Se Qayamat Tak* confirmed Aamir's status as the next big star, and boosted Juhi Chawla's career too. It also marked the beginning of a new era in melody, as each song became a rage, propelling music directors Anand-Milind and singer Udit Narayan to fame, and giving Alka Yagnik some of her early hits. Even today, '*Papa kehte hain*', '*Ae mere humsafar*', '*Gazab ka hai din*' and '*Akele hain toh kya gham hai*' are hummed by film music buffs. '*Gazab ka hai din*' is specially remembered for its picturisation on Aamir and Juhi under rows of trees.

Facing page: Enjoying himself while playing the drums.

Many would rightly believe *Qayamat Se Qayamat Tak* was Aamir's biggest musical success. If one looks at setting a new trend, attaining mass popularity or achieving commercial success, it was a landmark score. Moreover, it was just the beginning. Over the years, many of his movies have had outstanding music. Like Dev Anand, Rajesh Khanna and Amitabh Bachchan in their prime, or Shahrukh Khan later, Aamir almost always had some great songs picturised on him.

If one correlates Aamir's career graph with the music from his films, certain points become obvious. One is that though many playback singers sang for him, Udit Narayan and Kumar Sanu were used most regularly. The next point is that his films contained some of the most popular hits of the past twenty-five years. What's also notable is that some of his biggest hit songs were composed by specific music directors during different periods of his career. If we include his appearance as a child star in the title song of the 1973 film *Yaadon Ki Baaraat*, we could begin with R.D. Burman. Much later, there have been many music directors who have done only one Aamir film. We shall cover them later in this article.

We begin by concentrating initially on those composers who consistently created songs for him. We can divide them into various periods, clubbing some of them who worked around the same time.

The famous 'Aati kya Khandala' *song with Rani Mukherjee where Aamir did playback singing for the first time.*

Aamir dancing to the song 'Nasha Yeh Pyar' *from the film* Mann.

The most prominent ones, in chronological order, with the years denoting the time they worked for Aamir's films are as follows:

- Anand-Milind: 1988–1991
- Bappi Lahiri: 1989–1995
- Nadeem-Shravan: 1991–1996
- Jatin-Lalit: 1992–2006
- Anu Malik: 1995–2000
- A.R. Rahman: 1996–2008
- Shankar-Ehsaan-Loy: 2001–2009

Let us now analyse them in detail:

Of the music directors, the first few years were clearly dominated by Anand-Milind and Bappi Lahiri. The former, who got a *Filmfare* award for *Qayamat Se Qayamat Tak*, later worked in the hugely popular *Dil* (co-starring the gorgeous Madhuri Dixit and featuring the hits '*Mujhe neend na aaye*' and '*Khambe jaisi khadi hai*'. The other films of Aamir for which the duo created music were *Deewana Mujh Sa Nahin* (known for its title track) and the less successful *Tum Mere Ho, Jawani Zindabad* and *Daulat Ki Jung*.

For his part, Bappi composed for *Love Love Love, Awwal Number, Isi Ka Naam Zindagi, Aatank Hi Aatank* and *Afsana Pyar Ka*, the last one being known for the hit '*Tip tip baarish*', sung by Amit Kumar (the musical genius Kishore Kumar's son) and Asha Bhosle. Interestingly, while Anand-Milind preferred Udit after their initial success, Bappi was more in favour of Amit and even experimented with Vijay Benedict, in *Love Love Love*. Vijay had sung 'I am a Disco Dancer' for Mithun Chakraborty's cult film *Disco Dancer* (1982).

Both these duos, Nadeem-Shravan and Jatin-Lalit, came out with excellent music for Aamir Khan. Nadeem-Shravan had a huge musical success with the 1991 release *Dil Hai Ke Manta Nahin*. The title song, '*Kaise mizaaj aapke hain*' and '*Adaayen bhi hain, mohabbat bhi hai*', both sung by Kumar Sanu and Anuradha Paudwal, and filmed on Aamir and Pooja Bhatt touched the hearts of the audience. From the same film, '*Tu pyaar hai kisi aur ka*' was also hugely popular, though it was a rehash of Ghazal maestro Mehdi Hassan's '*Main khayal hoon kisi aur ka*'.

Nadeem-Shravan had two other enormous achievements for the actor. The Aamir-Juhi Chawla film *Hum Hain Rahi Pyar Ke* (1993) had the hits '*Ghunghat ki aad se dilbar ka*', '*Yun hi kat jaayega safar*' and '*Mujhse mohabbat ka izhaar*' (Kumar Sanu and Alka Yagnik), besides '*Chikni soorat tu kahaan*' (Kumar Sanu and chorus). Alka Yagnik won the National Award for Best Female Playback Singer in 1994 for this film. Three years later, *Raja Hindustani* with co-star Karisma Kapoor had '*Poocho zara poocho*' (Alka-Sanu), '*Pardesi pardesi*' (three versions), '*Aaye ho meri zindagi mein*' (separate versions by Udit and Alka) and '*Kitna pyara tujhe rab ne banaya*' (Alka-Udit), which was inspired by Nusrat Fateh Ali Khan's '*Kinna sona tenu rab ne banaya*'.

As for Jatin-Lalit, they in fact produced one of the best songs of the actor's career—the melodious '*Pehla nasha*' from *Jo Jeeta Wohi Sikandar*. Rendered by Udit Narayan and Sadhana Sargam, Majrooh Sultanpuri's lyrics '*Pehla nasha, pehla khumaar, naya pyaar hai, naya intezaar, kar loon mein kya apna haal, aye dil-e-beqaraar, mere dil-e-beqaraar, tu hi bata*' remain relevant even today. The effervescent dreamy-eyed joy of Aamir and Ayesha Jhulka is impossible to forget. It has become a quintessential romantic song through time and a favourite of music lovers. The movie also had the anthemic '*Yahaan ke hum sikandar*'.

Jatin-Lalit went on to compose music for three more popular movies of Aamir. In 1998, *Ghulam* had the super hit '*Aati kya Khandala*', in which the actor himself sang in a spoken style and Alka Yagnik was the voice for Rani Mukherjee. The song received instant prominence. The following year, the music of *Sarfarosh* had the peppy tracks '*Iss deewane ladke ko*' and the sensually romantic '*Jo haal dil ka*' with the beautiful Sonali Bendre dancing with Aamir. But the film's biggest hits were Jagjit Singh's '*Hoshwalon ko khabar kya*', picturised on Naseeruddin Shah (featuring Aamir in some shots), and Sonu Nigam's '*Zindagi maut na ban jaaye*' used in the opening credits.

Then after a long gap, Jatin-Lalit composed for an Aamir film in *Fanaa*, released in 2006. This was also the brothers' last film as a duo. The lyrics of Prasoon Joshi were refreshing and Shaan sang '*Chand sifaarish*', with Kailash Kher providing the background vocals as Aamir serenades Kajol, playing a blind girl, at a Delhi tourist spot. In '*Mere haath mein tera haath ho*' and '*Dekho na*', Sonu Nigam and Sunidhi Chauhan mesmerised the listeners with their soulful voice.

In the second half of the 1990s, Anu Malik was arguably the most prolific composer on the scene, though some of his songs were inspired by popular foreign songs too. His stint with Aamir began with *Baazi* and *Akele Hum Akele* Tum in 1995 and ended with *Mela* in 2000.

Baazi had the popular Udit Narayan-Sadhana Sargam song '*Dheere dheere aap mere dil ke mehmaan ho gaye*', which was reworked from Mehdi Hassan's

With Twinkle Khanna in a scene from Mela.

'*Rafta rafta woh meri hasti ka saamaan ho gaye*'. Anu copied Western classical musician Beethoven's '*Fur elise*' to create '*Jaane mujhe kya hua*'. The film also had Aamir dressed as a woman on '*Dole dole dil dole*', which was a direct lift of the international hit '*Come September*'.

Akele Hum Akele Tum, co-starring Manisha Koirala, had a successful title song, besides '*Raja ko rani se pyaar ho gaya*' (based on the main theme of the classic 1972 film, *The Godfather*) and '*Dil mera churaya kyon*' (a remake of pop group Wham's '*Last Christmas*').

Ishq, Anu's 1997 film with Aamir, had some pleasing numbers like '*Neend churayee meri*', '*Humko tumse pyaar hai*', '*Ishq hua, kaise hua*' and '*Mr Lova Lova*', replicated from the well-known reggae pop star Shaggy's '*Mr Lova

Lova'. In *Mela*, the music director shared credits with Rajesh Roshan and Leslie Lewis, but his songs '*Mela dilon ka*' and '*Tujhe rab ne banaya kamaal*' were well received.

If Anand-Milind, Nadeem-Shravan and Jatin-Lalit ruled the music in the first half of Aamir's career, the second half clearly belonged to A.R. Rahman. It began with Ram Gopal Varma's 1996 film *Rangeela*, with Udit singing for Aamir on '*Kya karein kya na karein*' and '*Yaaro sun lo zara*'. This was the first Hindi film for which Rahman composed music and he received a *Filmfare* award for it. Two years later, in Deepa Mehta's *Earth*, Sukhwinder Singh's harmonious '*Rut aa gayee re*' and the haunting '*Raat ki daldal hain*' are accompanied by Srinivas' heart-wrenching '*Yeh jo zindagi hain*' (two versions). The songs are situational and enhance the mood of the film.

Rahman's biggest musical success with Aamir was undoubtedly Ashutosh Gowariker's *Lagaan* in 2001, which had lyrics by Javed Akhtar. The film based on cricket re-established Udit Narayan's talent when it came to singing for Aamir, as he rendered the brilliantly choreographed '*Ghanan ghanan*' (where villagers wait for the onset of rain), '*Mitwa*', '*Radha kaise na jale*' and '*O re chhori*'. Here, Aamir and Gracy Singh showed great on-screen chemistry whenever they appeared together. In the motivational team song, '*Chale chalo*', Rahman himself did the playback. The eathy music along with the lyrics managed to capture the local flavour of the village, its condition, people's emotions and their uncertain future. Even though it was a period film, the music appealed to all.

When Aamir returned to the silver screen in 2005, the ace composer teamed up with him by giving the score of another period film *Mangal Pandey: The Rising*. With Javed Akhtar's thoughtful lyrics, Rahman meticulously created compositions for this film. The theme music, '*Mangal Mangal*' is evocatively chanted by Kailash Kher and is followed by two more versions of it called '*Agni*' and '*Aatma*', the last one being rendered along with Sukhwinder Singh. A *mujra* with an irresistible tune and the intense vocals of Kavita Krishnamurthy and Reena Bharadwaj is undeniably the best track of the film. A qawwali '*Al Maddath Maula*' in Rahman's inimitable voice is great to listen to and an added bonus in the soundtrack.

In a jubilant mood in the title track from Rang De Basanti.

The Rahman-Aamir duo returned with a bang in 2006 with *Rang De Basanti*. The album opens with a holy chant (*gurbani*) '*Ik Onkar*' with Harshdeep Kaur's mellifluous voice. It is followed by the title track '*Rang de basanti*' sung by Daler Mehndi and penned by Prasoon Joshi, which starts off with a typical bhangra chorus but pounding beats of rock music and electronic instrumentation blend in this song to create a lilting melody. Chithra's part in the song is short but magnificent. This gives way to a foot-tapping, energetic song '*Paathshala*' for the young generation with Naresh Iyer and Mohammed Aslam providing the vocals and Aamir dancing in his unique style. It starts off as a techno track but becomes a mix of various genres at the end. Another version of this song '*Paathshala* (Be a Rebel)' with rap from Blaaze also became quite popular. '*Tu bin bataye*' by Madhushree is a slow-paced song that is a soothing balm for the mind and is in complete contrast to the previous song. The sweet lullaby is soon replaced by the song '*Khalbali*' containing elements of the Middle East in it and sung by Arabic singer Nacim with Rahman and Mohammed Aslam. Mohit Chauhan does a fantastic job in the soft song '*Khoon Chala*' that has very powerful lyrics. All the songs are superbly captured on reel. Rahman sings a duet '*Luka Chuppi*' with the veteran Lata Mangeshkar and this is probably the highest point of this soundtrack. Its emotionally overpowering lyrics stay with you for long. The last song '*Rubaroo*' is the icing on the cake with Naresh Iyer accompanying Rahman to create an instantly hummable, peppy and iconic track. The variations in the music of this film are just an example of the sheer genius of A.R. Rahman.

In 2008, Aamir did *Ghajini* for which Rahman gave the music. It had the Sonu Nigam-Javed Ali hit '*Guzaarish*', with Aamir and Asin captured in a breathtaking outdoor sequence. '*Kaise Mujhe*' is a purely romantic song by Benny Dayal and Shreya Ghoshal. Among the catchy songs are '*Aye Bachchu*' sung in an uninhibited style by Suzanne D'Mello, while '*Latoo*' is an upbeat dance number sung by Shreya Ghoshal. One of the best songs in this album is '*Behka*' sung splendidly by Karthik. The music is a harmonious mix of hip-hop, pop and jazz styles, while the instruments produce a wonderful medley.

Rahman also worked in *Jaane Tu... Ya Jaane Na* in 2008, co-produced by Aamir that starred his nephew Imran and the bubbly Genelia D'Souza. Its music was considered innovative and fresh, holding the number one spot on the music charts for several weeks. '*Kabhi Kabhi Aditi*' by Rashid Ali and '*Pappu Can't Dance*' by Benny Dayal, Mohammed Aslam, Blaaze, Anupama and other young singers were the major hits.

The musical trio of Shankar-Ehsaan-Loy gave its most path-breaking songs in Farhan Akhtar's *Dil Chahta Hai* in 2001. The film, also starring Saif Ali Khan, Preity Zinta and Akshaye Khanna, had many hit numbers. The ones picturised on Aamir included '*Jaane kyun*' sung by Udit Narayan and Alka Yagnik, which used the Australian instrument didgeridoo, and Sonu Nigam's pathos-filled '*Tanhayee*'. The songs which had all the three stars were the extremely popular like '*Koi kahe kehta rahe*' sung by Shankar Mahadevan, Shaan and KK, and '*Dil Chahta Hai*' sung by Shankar Mahadevan and Clinton Cerejo. This music album was a landmark as it combined several styles of music to create an altogether novel sound, very different from the ordinary songs produced in those days.

Shankar-Ehsaan-Loy returned with Aamir in his directorial debut *Taare Zameen Par* in 2007. The sentimental and touching song '*Maa*' eloquently sung by Shankar Mahadevan and picturised on child star Darsheel Safary conveyed the insecurities of a child when sent away from home. The measured pace of title song '*Taare Zameen Par*' by Shankar Mahadevan takes us to a world with unlimited possibilities. Prasoon Joshi's heartfelt lyrics remind us of our childhood. The peppy '*Bam bam bole*' sung by Shaan along with Aamir was a fun song filmed on Aamir dressed like a clown to entertain the school kids. '*Jame Raho*' was a situational and imaginative track, while '*Mera Jahan*' containing a kid's chorus and Adnan Sami's soulful vocals gives us a view of the child protagonist's naive world.

Others: The earliest set of people to have worked in Aamir's films were Rajat Dholakia in *Holi* and Ranjit Barot in *Raakh*. Shiv-Hari chose singer Abhijeet and Lata Mangeshkar for the hit song '*Phoolon ke is sehar mein*' in *Parampara*. Among the other music directors, only two or three had hugely successful scores in the films done by Aamir. The first was Tushar Bhatia, who came out

At the music release of Yamla Pagla Deewana 2—*Sunny Deol (extreme left), Shahrukh Khan, Juhi Chawla embraced by Aamir, Neha Sharma and writer-director Kunal Kohli.*

with a superb collection in Rajkumar Santoshi's 1994 comedy *Andaz Apna Apna*. The songs picturised on Aamir included '*Ello ello*' and '*Dil karta hai*'.

Next came the duo Sanjeev-Darshan, sons of music director Shravan, banked entirely on Udit Narayan in *Mann*, who sang the songs '*Nasha yeh pyaar kai*', '*Mera mann*', '*Tinak tin taana*', '*Chaha hai tujhko*', '*Khushiyan aur gham*' with Alka Yagnik, Anuradha Paudwal accompanying him in the duet songs. Sameer had written the lyrics for the songs.

In 2009, Shantanu Moitra also struck gold by composing the music for Rajkumar Hirani's *3 Idiots* co-starring Kareena Kapoor, R. Madhavan and Sharman Joshi. Swanand Kirkire, the multitalented musician and lyricist wrote the apt, humorous and soulful words for the songs. The album had several super hits sung by Sonu Nigam like '*Aal izz well*' accompanied by Shaan and Swanand Kirkire, '*Zoobi doobi*' with Shreya Ghoshal, the heart-wrenching '*Jaane nahin denge tujhe*' and lastly Shaan's solo vocals on '*Behti hawa sa tha woh*'.

In 2010, the well-known Argentinian musician Gustavo Santaolalla gave the score in *Dhobi Ghat*. He had created the soundtracks of outstanding films like Alejandro González Iñárritu's *Amores Perros* (2000), *21 Grams* (2003), *Babel* (2006), *Biutiful* (2010); Walter Salles' *The Motorcycle Diaries* (2004); Ang Lee's *Brokeback Mountain* (2005) and many more. The popular fusion music band Indian Ocean did a few songs in Aamir's production *Peepli (Live)*. Of the forthcoming films of Aamir, Pritam is working on *Dhoom 3: Back in Action* and Amar Mohile in *P.K.*

Recently, however, Ram Sampath has been doing some great work for Aamir. He did a remix in *Peepli (Live)*, but his real association began with *Delhi Belly*, which Aamir co-produced. It had some lively songs like '*Bhaag D.K. Bose*', '*Ja Chudail*', '*Bedardi Raja*' and '*Switty Tera Pyaar Chaida*' with naughty lyrics teetering on the border of obscenity, but were quite popular among the current generation. Among other tunes, Ram composed '*I hate you (like I love you)*', where Aamir did a special appearance in flashy clothes and monster-sized goggles reminiscent of the disco era.

Ram's big break, of course, was the Aamir-anchored TV series *Satyamev Jayate*, where he composed the title track and the theme-based songs that appeared at the end of each episode. At that point, he also did the music for Reema Kagti's *Talaash* (2012). It had the songs '*Muskaanein Jhooti Hai*' that had a retro feel to it sung by Suman Sridhar, '*Jiya laage na*' sung splendidly by Sona Mohapatra and Ravindra Upadhyay and the edgy '*Jee le zaraa*' by Vishal Dadlani.

To sum up, Aamir has had an amazing musical innings ever since *Qayamat Se Qayamat Tak* was released. He himself is a diehard music lover. I remember seeing him in the Mangal Pandey garb for a concert by his favourite rock band Jethro Tull at Mumbai's Homi Bhabha Auditorium nine years ago. And yes, he also played Beethoven's '*Fur elise*' on the piano during a TV show and joined in on drums with the band Indian Ocean at the *Peepli (Live)* music launch.

Aamir holding Madhuri's hand lovingly in a scene from Dil.

Naturally, Aamir has a wonderful ear for music, and those close to him talk about the attention he pays to the quality of the songs. The result is very evident for all his fans to hear.

Narendra Kusnur is a Mumbai-based music columnist and critic.

TAKE TWO

TURNING TO MEANINGFUL CINEMA AND DIRECTION

'Films have a life of their own. It's like a wild horse. If you're not able to control it, it takes you for a ride.'

CAFE

In a reflective pose during a special photo session for Dil Chahta Hai.

Facing page: A still from Dil Chahta Hai *where Aamir had spiky hair and a soul patch.*

The year 2001 had its share of good and bad moments for Aamir. While his first production *Lagaan* achieved tremendous success, he got separated from his first wife Reena in the same year. Whereas the success of *Lagaan* and *Dil Chahta Hai* provided him a lot of strength and reinforced his belief in himself, his divorce shattered him to the core. Between 2001 and 2005, Aamir did not sign a single film and he was not even listening to scripts; it was a traumatic period of his life. 'When I went through the separation with Reena, I realised that I was emotionally and mentally not in a state to work. So I stopped working,' he stated in his interview to *M* magazine. He was thankful that he did not have to complete the shoot of any film signed earlier; his resolution of concentrating on one project at a time worked in his favour. He was least bothered if people would remember him or not; all he knew that he was not capable of working in that phase of his life.

Aamir completely immersed himself into the character of Mangal Pandey.

Right: A photo shoot for Mangal Pandey *in Ketan Mehta's office that took place past midnight.*

His only concern at that time was his children. 'I wanted to devote all the time I got with them to ... just being with them, holding them, reassuring them. So I didn't even move around; I was at home all the time,' he revealed in the same interview.

Aamir in his look from Mangal Pandey, *twirling his moustache to perfection.*

So what made Aamir end his sabbatical and return to films? Aamir, who had always given first preference to directors while choosing films, could not say no to Ketan Mehta when he approached him in 2003 once again. The actor, whose second criteria to choose a film had been a good script, liked the story that Ketan narrated to him. It was a period film and totally different from the first film that he had offered him when Aamir was a teenager. 'The concept of a company ruling a country was fascinating for me. The events might have happened in 1857, but the issues are very relevant, even today,' Aamir mentioned in an interview. The film essentially explored the concept of freedom and questioned the right of any one society's power to move into someone else's society and take it over. No matter what made him choose Ketan Mehta's film *Mangal Pandey: The Rising*, it was evident that the actor was now in his own space. He was now in a position to pick and choose what he liked on his own terms.

After signing the film, he immersed himself completely into the character of Mangal Pandey, India's first freedom fighter. Though there were hardly any records about Mangal, a lot of information was recorded about that period, which helped Aamir understand the time in which the story was set. 'I went into only a fraction, but it gave me a sense of the time,' Aamir recalled and also added, 'This film uses Mangal as a symbol of freedom who represents that section of the Indian society that had begun to question and rise.' When the film was announced it stirred the trade circles, since Aamir had signed a film after a long break.

Aamir lived the character of a sepoy during the making of this film. The long hair, the moustache and the turban became a part of him even off camera. Though it was a tough project, Aamir stayed committed to it entirely for three years. During those days, he also did a commercial for Titan watches donning the same look. No matter what, he refused to change the look till the last shot of the film was canned. 'It was a very tough film to be a part of. A demanding film, but at the end of the day, a very satisfying experience,' he stated.

Since the film was announced, people were eagerly awaiting its release. His fans were desperate to find out what their favourite entertainer had to offer them this time. Somewhere during the same time in the previous year, the Shahrukh Khan starrer *Veer-Zaara* was also released. Yash Raj Films distributed both these films. Though *Mangal Pandey* was not considered a successful film, its initial box-office collections were better than *Veer-Zaara*, which was revealed much later. However, Aamir was least affected by such trade habits; he was proud of his film. After a few years in a television show *Aap Ki Adalat*, Aamir revealed that *Mangal Pandey* did two to three times more business than many of his other successful films. In the same show Aamir also pondered on the reasons for the failure of the film. He felt one of the reasons could be that the film failed to establish an emotional connect with the audience. Indians being passionately patriotic wanted to see the British, who ruled and oppressed them for several years, being thrashed in the film. However, Aamir could not change the end of the movie based on historical events and thus his character had to be hanged in the end, which the audience may not have liked.

Real vs Reel—Aamir posing with a large cardboard cut-out from his film Mangal Mandey.

Aamir was now in a stage of his career where the commercial success or failure of a film was not a matter of serious concern for him; all that mattered was that the projects he was associated with made him happy and content. His next two films *Rang De Basanti* (*RDB*) and *Fanaa* in 2006 established him as a versatile actor to reckon with. While he played a fun-loving, Delhi-based youngster's character in the former, he convincingly essayed the role of a ruthless assassin in the latter. Audiences loved him in

Rehan (Aamir), the tourist guide with Zooni (Kajol) in Fanaa.

both these roles and appreciated the ease with which he could play a positive as well as a negative role. Both films reflected the social ills of the period and how it could be handled to find a solution.

When he signed *Rang De Basanti*, he knew that four films had already been made on the story of freedom fighters Bhagat Singh and Chandrashekhar Azad and none had been successful. When Aamir told his sister in New York about his new project she was surprised and warned him about his decision. But Aamir was determined to take the risk as he liked the script where the modern protagonists and their inspirations were placed in line with the period story of Indian freedom fighters. In Aamir's words, the film was about the youth of today and their lack of involvement in the current social and political issues.

Rakeysh Omprakash Mehra, the director of the film commented on Aamir's sensibility as an actor, 'I never had to tell him how to shoot a scene. All I had to tell him was what not to do. There was a shot in *RDB* where R. Madhavan dies in a plane crash and Aamir had to break down. It was to be shot on Monday. Aamir spent the entire weekend preparing for it. But on Monday, I didn't feel

emotionally prepared to shoot it. I couldn't imagine his "breakdown". I thought about it for two to three days. ... And when we shot the scene, Aamir was crying in front of the camera and I behind it.' The film's box-office success was a reflection of the fact that it stirred the feelings of pride and anger in the hearts of the audience. It rarely happens that a film can shake the conscience of the audience in such a way that they leave the theatres with a will to do something to change themselves as well as their society. Films like *Rang De Basanti* are rarely made and Rakeysh won the *Filmfare* Best Director Award for his groundbreaking efforts.

With Sonali Bendre in a romantic scene from Sarfarosh.

Facing page: Sporting the Rang De Basanti *look.*

The nihilism depicted in the film started debates while its emotional activism provoked candlelight marches. Though the impact of all these movements faded after some time, Aamir's character in the film remains memorable. To all this, Aamir's only reaction was, 'So nice.' An eighty-five-minute documentary called *Ru-Ba-Ru* has been made about the film's impact on the country. It revolves round a group of carefree friends, who turn rebellious and take on the government in a drastic manner to make a point against increasing corruption in India. It captures real-life incidents, which also highlights the concerns touched upon in the movie—be it the candlelight protest to get Jessica Lal's murderer convicted or the protests led by Anna Hazare. Mehra himself participated in the demonstrations against the recommendation and implementation of the Mandal Commission by former prime minister, V.P. Singh, back in 1989. The recollections of those troubled times played an important role when Mehra was making *Rang De Basanti*.

Aamir is a pro in the art of moulding himself to suit the character, irrespective of what it takes. In *Fanaa*, Aamir who is known to bring something new to his character in every film, donned two different looks and was equally convincing in both. Aamir

KALPANA AS KILLED
WHO

strongly believes that the responsibility of a creative person is much more than entertaining the audience. It extends to building the fabric of society by inculcating values in people. He feels he has a job to raise the sensitivity of people about social issues. This belief of his had grave repercussions on the commercial success of his film in Gujarat. Due to his anti-Narmada Dam remarks, the release of his film *Fanaa*, directed by Kunal Kohli, was stalled for some time in Gujarat. But Aamir refused to budge from his decision and maintained his stand on the Narmada Dam issue. As he believed that he had done nothing wrong by expressing his thoughts about this issue, he was determined not to apologise for his comments to anyone. Finally when the movie released in some theatres of Gujarat, it did register some business.

In his Ghajini *look with Salman Khan on the sets of* 10 Ka Dum *to promote his film.*

Facing page: Aamir worked very hard to get this chiselled look and eight-pack abs for Ghaijni.

Aamir has always been fully committed to his films, which talks highly about his professionalism. This quality of Aamir is specially praised by his directors. Rakeysh Omprakash Mehra asserted, 'He makes himself completely accessible to the filmmaker.' Kunal Kohli seconds him by adding, 'He's there whether it is for readings or costume trials.' Kunal fondly recalled that Aamir was apologetic for requesting him for four days leave in the middle of the shoot in Mumbai in 2005 since he wanted to get married to Kiran Rao. Apart from his obligations, Kunal also admires Aamir for his intellect, '... he's just incredibly intelligent. How many people do you know who can solve the Rubik's cube with one hand?'

As an actor, the two outstanding films of his in recent years have been *Ghajini*, a psychological thriller and *3 Idiots*, a comedy-drama. The way in which the star prepared himself to present to the world in the two movies was admirable. He silenced his critics and staunch rivals with the techniques he employed to portray his characters in these two films. The greatness of his efforts can be measured by the fact that when actor Akshay Kumar, in the same year, was awarded a trophy in the popular actor category, he refused to accept the award saying that it really belonged to Aamir for his

Appreciating the greeting cards presented to him by the children of The Druk White Lotus School in Leh, Ladakh where a part of 3 Idiots *was shot.*

performance in *Ghajini*. Salman Khan went to Aamir's house to personally congratulate him for his mind-blowing performance in this film. When other actors were proudly flaunting their six packs, Aamir came to the forefront with his eight packs and well-built body. Salman, who is known for his great body fitness appreciated Aamir for his eight-pack abs. Aamir worked hard to build his body not to compete as a fitness freak, but to bring credibility to his performance. Today when words of praise are showered upon him, he believes that his hard work has paid off. Imran Khan, the actor's nephew in an interview to *HT Café* said, 'It's remarkable that in so many years, Aamir has managed to underplay himself and iconise his characters in his movies.'

Apoorva Lakhia who worked with Aamir as a chief aide in *Lagaan* said to *Stardust* magazine in April 2009, 'Aamir Khan is the only actor in India that audiences trust. An Aamir film will always get a fantastic opening. It is a difficult thing to make a billion people trust you but Aamir makes that happen.' Aamir's talent proved that the actor never needed big filmmakers to support him to get success.

Posing against a poster of 3 Idiots *with a wide smile.*

Launch of meaningful cinema with Aamir Khan Productions

It was *Lagaan* that forced Aamir to get his act together to become a producer. But he was not just a one-time producer and wanted to keep his banner afloat. Aamir had learnt a great deal of filmmaking from his uncle and father. He was proud of Indian cinema and stood up for it when needed but realised that substandard films with weak scripts were also a part of this very same cinema. Since then he pledged to make different but meaningful cinema under his production banner.

Once Aamir Khan Productions was launched, it was time to introduce new directors. Amole Gupte and his wife Deepa Bhatia were developing a story as a way of comprehending why some children could not accustom themselves to the traditional education system. Initially a short story called 'High Jump', it developed into a screenplay for a film over several years. In an interview to *The Hindu* in 2008, Deepa claimed that her initial idea was not dyslexia but the childhood of the legendary Japanese filmmaker Akira Kurosawa, whose performance in school at first was unsatisfactory, until he started excelling after meeting an enlightened art teacher who transformed his life. In their research regarding the underperformance of young children, Amole and Deepa kept posing issues like: what was wrong with them? Were they slow learners, disinterested or incapable? Their search for the answers led them to meet several teachers, parents and special educators like Kate Currawalla of the Maharashtra Dyslexia

Above: In an emotional scene with Darsheel Safary from Taare Zameen Par.

Below: A painting by Samir Mondal for Taare Zameen Par.

Association and Medha Loltikar of PACE (Parents' Association for Appropriate Education of the Child). On interacting with these special teachers, Amole and Deepa were sensitised to the world of children. Finally, dyslexia became the focal point of the film and the duo gained first-hand experience of the troubles, anxieties and joys that the kids with learning difficulties faced in school. Amole Gupte conducted several art and drama workshops with the children and got to know them better. He figured out how their minds functioned and discovered most of them thought 'out of the box', a quality that he admired the most.

Aamir with Salman in an action sequence from Andaz Apna Apna.

Amole Gupte's compelling story of a dyslexic child became the story of the film *Taare Zameen Par* (*TZP*). When Aamir heard the story, it stirred an unrestrained feeling within him, which he wanted to share with everyone and thus, decided to produce the film. He knew that the subject was unheard of, there was no heroine in the film and the main lead was a child; all these factors would be enough for any producer to back out but Aamir was not the one to do so. When people got to know about his new project, they questioned him if he was making a documentary as the subject had not been dealt in commercial cinema before. Many people did not even know what dyslexia was all about.

During the making of this film, the producer and director had major differences of opinion and the team broke off. Though Amole Gupte had all the freedom to make this film with someone else, he asked Aamir to direct it. Yes, directing films was on Aamir's mind, even before he wanted to become an actor, but finally he took up the responsibility in 2007 with *Taare Zameen Par*. Beyond the world of authenticity and credibility, the film was an emotional overdrive that left all its viewers numb. This film was not just accurate; it was exceptionally effective in its storytelling. From the casting of Darsheel Safary as Ishaan to a perfect mix of comedy and drama, the film was worth every joyous tear and Aamir received rave reviews for it. After watching the movie, every child now dreams to have a teacher like Aamir—kind, supportive as well as fun to be with. He took special care of his look in the film to reflect all these shades of human nature. The film connected very well with the audience, especially families with such children. It had brought a change in people's attitude towards children and education. The film had not only affected the lives of the audience but Aamir himself. Aamir won the Gollapudi Srinivas Award, a national-level private award given to a first-time director in Indian cinema every year, for *Taare Zameen Par*. The award was started by the family of the young director Gollapudi Srinivas, who died on the ninth day of the shooting of his first film. Though Aamir does not go to award ceremonies, he took this one as a great honour bestowed upon him by the fraternity.

When Rakeysh Omprakash Mehra was asked to describe Aamir as an actor, director and producer he said, 'I have known Aamir as actor, friend and producer and seen each overlap. Being a director, I have seen him with utmost clarity as an actor and he is a slave to the story he has to tell, a devotee to the script and the director's vision. As a producer he is the master—the backbone—and gives his full support.' In fact, Salman Khan is credited with suggesting the movie's title to Aamir Khan when they both met at a party. On seeing the film, Lata Mangeshkar, the nightingale of India commented, 'I saw Aamir Khan's *Taare Zameen Par*. He is a good director and a very good actor. I regard him as a personal friend.'

Aamir with watercolour artist Samir Mondal from whom he learnt painting during the making of Taare Zameen Par.

While Aamir was winning accolades from all corners for his directorial debut, he was missing his *chachajaan* Nasir Hussain's blessings very much. Shammi Kapoor, with whom his uncle shared a warm relationship, was someone Aamir chose to fill this void. On the music release of *Taare Zameen Par*, Aamir went to Shammi*ji*'s South Mumbai home with the music team. Aamir later said, '*Chachajaan* is not with us today but it would have been a very happy day for him. I wanted Shammi uncle to hear the music and wanted his blessings. Shammi uncle is the coolest and I so enjoyed being with him. Very few people have the spirit of life that Shammi uncle has and there is a lot to learn from him. He showed me a picture that he keeps in his room of him and *chachajaan* on the sets of one of the films they did together. I felt so happy.' With *Taare Zameen Par*, Aamir has become a complete entertainer; he had honed his talent as an actor and added some more value to his production house. But there were new milestones for him to conquer.

Aamir invited artist Samir Mondal to stay with him during Taare Zameen Par *so he could learn the finer nuances of a painter.*

While he was making innovative and touching films like *Lagaan* and *Taare Zameen Par*, he also produced a light-hearted film *Jaane Tu... Ya Jaane Na* (*JTYJN*) to launch his nephew Imran Khan. In this film he again dealt with the old concept of 'friendship develops into love' in a fresh manner, which was highly appreciated by the audience. So why did Aamir choose this film to launch his nephew? Well there are several twists in the story behind the making of this film. The film was earlier to be produced by Jhamu Sughand but since he ran into financial troubles and had to stall the project, it came to Aamir accidentally. Though his nephew was well aware of the success of his uncle's production house, he was not sure if Aamir would like to produce a romcom like *JTYJN* and thus asked his uncle to introduce him and his director Abbas Tyrewala to someone at UTV Productions, who were at that time producing *Rang De Basanti*. Aamir asked them to narrate the story to him. On listening to the story and the songs they created for the film, Aamir agreed to produce it but there was a catch. They had to wait for a year as at that time Aamir was committed to *Taare Zameen Par*. One year is never a big time for any director or actor when they know that Aamir is with them. Once the film released, everyone knew that their wait had paid off. It also spoke highly about Aamir's professionalism that did not change even

Aamir with the Delhi Belly *team.*

for his family members. When it came to work—Aamir was the same for everyone.

As a producer, for Aamir it is not satisfying only to produce successful films but equally important to create awareness in the society about social ills through the entertainment that his films offer. One such good example where societal issues were well amalgamated with entertainment was Anusha Rizvi's film *Peepli (Live)*. It was about the growing divide between rural and urban India. This film was unique in many ways. It had no renowned commercial actors of the industry besides Raghuveer Yadav; the rest of the cast were theatre actors and localities. It was not easy to make such a film, especially when you are targeting the audience world over. Aamir held several discussions with his team on how the film could be presented to the world. In one of the marathon meetings, an assistant got so fed up with those long discussions that he said in exasperation, 'Aamir it is such a small film, no stars, no cast and we are debating on it.' At first, Aamir went silent and then he told everyone that if they felt the film was really so bad, they were free to step out but he would still promote the film.

Aamir believed in the narrative and wished to support it. It may not have been an entertainer from any commercial standard but it had a tale. He was supporting it, even if it would be a flop. He created awareness about the film with a lot of conviction. This comic satire or black comedy, which sensitised the audience about the problems of rural India, was equally appreciated by the masses and classes. It garnered rave reviews from both the general audience and critics. Our Prime Minister, Dr Manmohan Singh, took time out from his busy schedule and watched the film. He

Aamir and his nephew Imran Khan with Shenaz Treasurywala (centre) at a promotional event for Delhi Belly.

A scene from Jo Jeeta Wohi Sikandar *depicting 'love at first sight' between Aamir and Ayesha Jhulka.*

praised director Anusha and her team for their valiant effort. He believed that the film spoke about issues, which are important to all of us. He also found the film very thought provoking and thus urged the industry to make more of such films. The film became India's official entry to the Oscars in the Best Foreign Language Film category that year and also got selected for the Sundance Film Festival.

Delhi Belly was the next film to come from Aamir Khan's production house. Totally contemporary in its feel, it featured Imran Khan with two new actors, Kunaal Roy Kapur and Vir Das. The director, Abhinay Deo, had made a below average film before this. Many believed that there was not much content in the film and the critics and rivals panned it. They questioned as to how a superstar like Aamir could be associated with such a bizarre film, full of obscene language and excessive adult content. But Aamir shut everyone up as the film was a hit all the way! Even the much controversial song '*Bhaag D.K. Bose*' was an instant ringer. On the success of *Delhi Belly*, Imran, the lead actor of the film said, 'I never thought *Delhi Belly* would be a box-office success. You can never get a fix on what the audiences want to watch.'

Among the film reviewers, Nikhat Kazmi of *The Times of India* wrote, 'All in all, *Delhi Belly* is a fine example of how the brightest and the boldest, when they pool in their talent, can create a film that is guaranteed to give you your money's worth, even as it re-writes all the moth-balled rules of an ageing industry. Enjoy the experience.' The film critic in *The Telegraph* praised writer Akshat Verma's 'original screenplay, which knows the difference between physical comedy and slapstick humour.' Taran Adarsh, a noted film trade analyst, wrote 'Eventually, *Delhi Belly* works big time predominantly for the reason that it's a pioneering motion picture, an incredible film that dares to pierce into an untapped and brand new terrain. The unblemished, racy screenplay coupled with super performances and a chartbusting musical score will make it a winner all the way.' The movie also received high praise

Aamir and Katrina interacting with the media at the launch of the title track of Dhoom: 3 *called* 'Dhoom machale'.

from critics outside India like Lisa Tsering of *The Hollywood Reporter*, Kevin Thomas of *The Los Angeles Times* and Peter Bradshaw of *The Guardian*. There were negative reviews too but in no way could it overpower the positive ones.

What matters to Aamir is good work and he can go to any lengths for it. Thus, when he had to audition for a role in his wife Kiran Rao's directorial debut *Dhobi Ghat* (also called *Mumbai Diaries*), he showed no qualms. The film, which was also written by Kiran,

As the gutsy ACP Ajay Singh Rathod in Sarfarosh.

was a slice of life about four characters in Mumbai, and how their lives intersect. It was her tribute to the city. Aamir played the role of a painter. The film received a lukewarm response from the audience probably because it could neither be categorised as a commercial film filled with entertainment, nor could it be classified as an art film.

Upon release, the film received mostly positive reviews from critics. Bhawana Somaaya, senior editor of *Ticket Please* wrote that 'Rao portrays the drudgery and the magnificence of the city in unforgettable imageries'. She also added that 'There is no doubting that *Dhobi Ghat* is amongst the most significant films in the history of Indian cinema'. Mathures Paul of *The Statesman* noted, '*Dhobi Ghat* is part atmospheric portrait, part video diary that has enough heart-breaking moments you don't want to watch. But neither can you look away'. Mayank Shekhar of the *Hindustan Times* stated, 'Bombay is the centre of this film's attention. It's probably the only city in the world where so many classes so closely merge into a common river of sorrows, beauty or hope: unaware of how each affects the other every day. This film is first-rate tribute; it's visceral, I realize—both clichés for compliments. Nothing more appropriate comes to mind.' Some reviewers criticised the film's languid pace, its excess melancholic atmosphere, pretentiousness, dull moments and drifting storyline. In spite of all its flaws, it was quite a well-made film with great performances from all the actors.

Though Aamir realised that all the three films—*Peepli (Live)*, *Delhi Belly* and *Dhobi Ghat* were for a niche audience and thus, the risks involved were huge, he decided to produce them because he knew his audience well and had a plan to make these films economically viable. He made the films keeping the global audience in mind and also distributed them in that way. He used the term art-house to describe *Dhobi Ghat* because that is what he believed the film was and thus, wanted to be truthful to his audience, who had always shown immense faith in him.

Interacting with Shammi Kapoor who was very close to his uncle Nasir Hussain.

When it comes to Aamir, everything seems possible. Director Ram Gopal Varma (Ramu) went to the extent of comparing Aamir with God. He said, 'I called him God because Aamir's films right from *Lagaan*, *Taare Zameen Par* to *Delhi Belly* are so varied in mindset and themes and yet so successful. I've never witnessed Allah, Ram or Jesus do such a thing!'

His film *3 Idiots* is one of the highest grossers of the Indian film industry. This frothy, fun-filled, entertaining film cocktailed with social messages discussed the most important aspect of human life—self-actualisation. The film wildly entertained people, it was equally provocative and funny, and at the same time insightful as well. All these factors drew the audiences repeatedly to the theatres. The film questioned the present education system which in an effort to enhance the performance of students was perhaps curtailing their innate intelligence and common sense. While the film raised several questions, it also provided answers through the characters of R. Madhavan, Sharman Joshi and Aamir. The film did not talk about winning at all costs; instead it gave hope to people that if you follow your heart, you will be happy and therefore achieve success. Though the film was made with a lot of subtlety, it had a strong impact on the viewer. We can still find people assuring themselves with the phrase '*All Izz Well*' (the message was put through a song in the movie) in the gravest of situations. The film strongly asked the viewers not to chase success but excellence, and in the process of chasing excellence success would surely follow. This motto formed the premise of this film.

Aamir believes that success is subjective and can be measured only by the achiever. 'The degree of your success can only be measured by you and you alone. That's the core message of the film,' Aamir told news anchor and Editor-in-chief, Times Now,

93

Aamir being welcomed to The Druk White Lotus School in Ladakh where the shooting of 3 Idiots *had taken place.*

Arnab Goswami during his chat on the television show *Frankly Speaking*. His character Rancho in *3 Idiots* joined college to learn and not to get a degree. Aamir himself is very much like this character. After his successful debut, he signed many films but was not happy with any of them. At that time he promised himself that he will follow his heart; even if that does not make him successful, at least he would be happy in doing the kind of work he likes. In the same chat show, Aamir said, 'I am a lot like Rancho. If I would have been chasing success, I wouldn't have done films like *Lagaan*, *Sarfarosh*, *Rang De Basanti*, *Taare Zameen Par* and many more.' All these films were unconventional and thus, involved huge risks.

While the effervescent, kind-hearted character of Rancho made you smile, he also made you commend his fidgety freethinking mind; he in his unique ways touched and changed many lives. The forty-four-year-old Aamir had brought out the juvenile buoyancy and vivacity of a college boy in his character with such conviction that no other actor of his age would have been capable of. Sharman Joshi and R. Madhavan had provided ample support to Aamir in the movie. Sharman needs a special mention for portraying the dramatic as well funny side of his character with utmost ease.

The film has a universal value which connected it to the world audience. On meeting Rajkumar Hirani, the writer-director of *3 Idiots* in an event organised by Anil Ambani of Reliance Entertainment, the veteran Hollywood auteur Steven Spielberg asked him, 'I have seen your movie *3 Idiots* three times. I like its humane and emotional undertones. How do you write?' Due to all these reasons many international studios are planning its remake. It was the first Hindi film, which was released with a whopping 900 prints in the Mainland China. In Taiwan, the film was also adapted into a stage musical.

Aamir in the suspense drama, Talaash.

Facing page: Aamir with the graceful Rani Mukherjee at the music launch of Talaash.

After *3 Idiots*, the actor produced a few films and was then seen as Inspector Surjan Singh Shekhawat in *Talaash*. This was the third time he was playing a policeman after *Baazi* and *Sarfarosh* but like always, he donned a different look—a handlebar moustache. Though there is a common perception in the Indian film industry that darker emotions do not make for good commercial cinema, Aamir chose to do the film on the first hearing itself as he found the story intriguing and engaging yet quite emotional.

Talaash once again brought together the trio of Aamir, Farhan Akhtar and Ritesh Sidhwani eleven years after the release of *Dil Chahta Hai*. The film was a suspense drama, which had many edge-of-the-seat scenes; it also dealt with various aspects of relationships. Aamir said to *Bombay Times*, 'It is easier to work with people who share the same level of passion for cinema that I have. They have also been a part of a few experimental films like me. I am glad with the way the film has turned out and I hope it opens new doors for suspense as a genre.' His wife Kiran loved *Talaash* and said, 'It is my kind of film. The story is such that everyone will get something in it. It is emotional so it should touch a chord with the audience and at the same time leads them to think as well.'

Like many others, Reema Kagti, the director of the film also had the best time working with Aamir. 'He was cool, chilled out

Looking cool in a bowler hat at the promo launch of Dhoom: 3.

and supportive. He's enthusiastic about the project, which is inspiring,' she stated in *HT Café*. While we keep hearing about Aamir being the interferer, Reema shared altogether a different experience. 'Once we agreed on the script, we stuck to it,' informed Reema. About his equation with Aamir, Farhan informed *Bombay Times*, 'His level of dedication and commitment to films remain the same.'

Aamir's favourite scene in the film is the one where his character cannot sleep at night and plays out alternative scenarios of how he could have prevented his son's death. Aamir said in an interview to *Screen* magazine, 'It was extremely traumatic to play this character, because losing a loved one to a tragic, untimely accident has been my biggest nightmare, my biggest fear. And when playing my character, I had to relive my biggest fear everyday because every moment that Shekhawat lives, the fact that he has lost someone is an underlying emotion.'

On his co-stars Rani Mukherjee and Kareena Kapoor, Aamir cheerfully told *Bombay Times*, 'I'm fortunate that I get to romance these two very beautiful girls. It can be distracting for me ... Also, I have had a fantastic work equation with both of them ... Both girls are lucky for me. They are both fantastic actresses and lovely human beings.' Aamir felt relaxed working with them, 'They are very sorted. Both love their work, but at the same time, they have a great sense of humour. And, they also keep the atmosphere on the sets charged and jovial.'

A part of the audience found *Talaash* slow but the film was a hit. 'I am pleased with the response we have got for it. I don't believe in ghosts and I have had no supernatural experiences. Then again I don't believe in Spiderman and Superman either but I am happy to watch those films,' said Aamir to *People* magazine.

A fan of Aamir Khan's films, Lata Mangeshkar said that his last offering *Talaash* was one of his best. 'I like the fact that Aamir

Shooting for Dhoom: 3 *in Chicago.*

attempts new kinds of roles and deals with different stories. He is deeply involved in every aspect of filmmaking and is particular. He doesn't compromise on anything, which is great for any film.' There is a dearth of such suspense movies. The veteran singer is all praises for Khan's co-actors in the film too. 'Although Rani had a small role, her performance was commendable. She is a good actor. For Kareena, this role was different from the ones she has done in the past. She played it excellently and very convincingly.'

Over the years, audience's expectation from Aamir has increased in manifold ways, which scares the actor. 'It is really scary what people have come to expect of me. When I do films like *Ghajini* (2008) or *3 Idiots* (2009), I'm more relaxed because it is more mainstream. And if the film turns out well, you get the sense that people will like it. However, when you do a *TZP*, *RDB* or *Talaash*, even if it comes out well, you do not know whether people will like it or not,' said Aamir to *Bombay Times*.

Aamir with co-star Abhishek Bachchan responding to queries at the promo launch of Dhoom: 3.

Now all eyes are set on Aamir's next project—*Dhoom: 3*. To portray the character of a thief, who is also a professional circus artiste, Aamir once again had to go through rigorous workout sessions. David Poznanter who trained Aamir for this role said, 'I am a professional circus artiste, coach and personal trainer. So I was assisting him in weight training as well as a circus coach.' The result is a leaner and chiselled Aamir. He revealed to *People* magazine, 'I play a gymnast in *Dhoom: 3* so I had to have a lean physique with single digit body fat percentage. I have been training for more than a year. And yes, Kiran also feels that I have not looked this good before.'

In 2012, Aamir began shooting for *Dhoom: 3* in downtown Chicago. As the shooting schedule was long, Aamir also took his wife Kiran and their eight-month-old son, Azad to Chicago. As the *Dhoom* films and bikes are synonymous, lots of them were seen during the filming of a scene of this new action-thriller. It was amazing to notice how the action master was explaining the scene to everyone with couple of small toys when suddenly Aamir, dressed in all black with a black hat, arrived on his black BMW bike and everybody's

A young Aamir with Sanjay Dutt at a party.

eye shifted to him. Aamir was seen sporting a never seen before hairstyle to go with his villainous role. While everyone was busy shooting the scene, Aamir was relaxing on a chair, wearing his reading glasses and enjoying a book on Mahatma Gandhi called *Gandhi: A Memoir* by William L. Shirer, as noticed by an onlooker Bidisha Roy. Katrina Kaif plays the leading lady, while Abhishek Bachchan and Uday Chopra are reprising their roles of Jai Dixit and Ali respectively. *Dhoom: 3* is set to release around Christmas 2013. Abhishek Bachchan, who is playing the role of ACP Jai Dixit for the third time in the action franchise while Aamir plays the main antagonist said, 'It's absolutely brilliant to be working with Aamir. You get to learn so much. He is so much fun on the sets. He is like a child on the sets; he is so involved and enthusiastic about everything.'

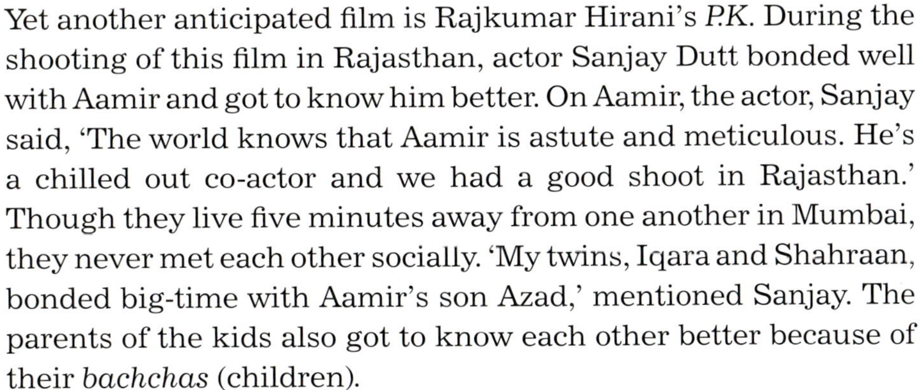

Yet another anticipated film is Rajkumar Hirani's *P.K.* During the shooting of this film in Rajasthan, actor Sanjay Dutt bonded well with Aamir and got to know him better. On Aamir, the actor, Sanjay said, 'The world knows that Aamir is astute and meticulous. He's a chilled out co-actor and we had a good shoot in Rajasthan.' Though they live five minutes away from one another in Mumbai, they never met each other socially. 'My twins, Iqara and Shahraan, bonded big-time with Aamir's son Azad,' mentioned Sanjay. The parents of the kids also got to know each other better because of their *bachchas* (children).

Over the years, Aamir has proved himself not only as an all-round performer but also as a marketing wizard. Aamir makes special efforts to promote all his films and his mind works round the clock on how to market it well. 'I always look for a foundational premise. I think that's crucial for a film's success. You must be able to sit back and reduce the idea of the film to one basic line,' he explained. Before the release of his films, no one would have any clue of what is going on in Aamir's head; it is always full of innovative ideas of how to communicate to his audience differently with each film. Thus, no one could even grasp the idea

Dancing with Kareena Kapoor in 3 Idiots.

when Aamir thought of bringing elephants to the music launch of *Mangal Pandey: The Rising* just to recreate the period and mood of the film. Though it could not happen due to lack of permissions, it never stopped Aamir from thinking aloud and different.

Aamir always thinks like a global star. He does not take on a project ad hoc but studies the subject and gets involved at every step of filmmaking. He puts the whole market and promotional blitzkrieg round the finished project and makes sure it is the talk of the town. That is the reason why all his projects post *Lagaan*, be it *RDB*, *3 Idiots*, *TZP* or *Dhobi Ghat* have all been felicitated at international film festivals and praised by the global audience as much as by the Indians.

He works in all possible ways to promote his films, but every time the means are different and yet so innovative, that it leaves marketing wizards wondering as to where he comes up with such plans from. For instance, when to oblige a friend's quest Aamir attended the premiere of Abbas-Mustan's film *Race*, where his look in *Ghajini* was seen for the first time, instantly people got curious to see his new avatar. Though this was not a planned move, it prompted Aamir to find out a unique way to promote this new look of his in this film. Thus, he cracked a deal with all multiplexes of India to make their staff don his unique *Ghajini* hairstyle. This strategic and intelligent move made people see Aamir's look in *Ghajini* everywhere and made it a popular topic of discussion.

His co-star in *Talaash* and *3 Idiots*, Kareena Kapoor considers herself fortunate to be working in back-to-back films with him. She has all praises for her favourite actor but does not find herself worthy enough to comment on Aamir's marketing strategies. 'He's a wizard in this field and we all know how a movie carries itself when his name is attached to it,' she told *Mid-Day*.

Though Aamir's unconventional marketing strategies, whether for his television show or his films, have always worked wonders, he hardly considers himself a 'marketing guru'. Such is the humility of this actor. He takes it as his responsibility and does everything to makes sure that people who are investing their hard-earned money in his projects earn good returns. But it has never affected the quality of his work. 'That doesn't mean I am compromising on my choice of work. But I am not the marketing guru that I am made out to be ... For me, reaching out to people is marketing. What I need to do for that comes organically,' described Aamir.

Today, most industry people feel that Aamir is at the helm of showbiz. There is no looking back for this actor who has metamorphosed into a 'complete superstar'. Amit Khanna, Chairman, Reliance Big Entertainment that distributed *3 Idiots*, believes that Aamir is a throwback to the Dilip Kumar-Raj Kapoor-Dev Anand era when filmmakers lived for cinema and believed it had a higher social purpose beyond making money. 'Yet he's as savvy as the new kids on the block, up to speed with (social media like) Facebook and blogging.' He is so bankable that

Mukesh Ambani, MD, Reliance Industries Limited (extreme left), Kamal Nath, Minister, Urban Development, Aamir Khan and Kumar Mangalam Birla, Chairman, Aditya Birla Group together at an award ceremony.

Aamir and Shahrukh at the Producer's Meet in 2009 to solve the revenue sharing issues between producers and exhibitors.

Apoorva Lakhia, his friend and first AD in *Lagaan* said, 'There is certain respectability in the Tata brand. When Ratan Tata brings out the Nano we know what to expect. Aamir enjoys a similar reputation. He is a reputed brand that never fails.'

Aamir feels that he is an unpredictable commodity who has no particular dynamic. Fortunately, that has also been his strength. 'The fact that people can't predict how much business my film is going to do or what grounds it will break is exciting. Even I cannot predict what my film is going to do. Experiencing the unknown has a certain charm to it,' he enthusiastically shared.

Though he has won several awards in the past for his films in various categories, he has been extremely selective in attending the award ceremonies in the last two decades, and he has his own reasons for it. Aamir, who always considered awards as an annual event where the industry got together and lauded each other's work, soon realised that the real purpose of awards were very different and thus decided to stay away from them. He thinks it is not possible to decide whether one performance is better than the other in a totally different context. 'Some 50,000 awards cropped up, everyone got one, and every year five new categories were added. It went live on TV. Now, it's not an award night, it's a programme designed to collect stars to generate advertisement time. I'm not interested in taking part in something like this. It's too childish for me. In the name of giving me an award, people are using me for TRP and to sell air-time,' expressed Aamir. Though he knows that his audience expects him to be a part of these shows and be accessible to them, without being arrogant, Aamir cannot do things he does not believe in.

Even after achieving so much success as actor, producer and director, Aamir has some unrealised dreams, which includes working with some ace directors of yesteryears like K. Asif, Guru Dutt, Bimal Roy, Mehboob Khan, V. Shantaram and Vijay Anand to name a few. We know that he would never be able to fulfil this dream but we surely know that the shades of the work of these great personalities have been seen and would be seen in his films as they have had a great influence on this filmmaker's mind. Aamir would also love to work with current actors Salman, Shahrukh, Akshay Kumar as well as with the great Amitabh Bachchan. He wishes someday, someone will cast all of them in a film.

Rajesh Khanna was referred to as the 'original superstar' of Indian cinema.

In a world of false diplomacy and evasiveness, Aamir is a straightforward man. A man of his word. His movies along with commercial successes, international acclaim convey important messages and are thought-provoking. His television show *Satyamev Jayate* was partly a talk show and partly journalism. All these virtues make Aamir the current face of Indian cinema. Though considered as an ageless actor, Aamir himself feels that an actor's peak time is about eight to ten years maximum and adds, 'Be it a female actor or a male actor, this is when they can make it. And they shine in that period. Everyone in the course of their time has their moment of sunshine. If it's me today, someone else will be there tomorrow.'

The last line spoken by Aamir Khan reminds us of the 'original superstar' Rajesh Khanna who would often recite this beautifully written line by poet Sahir Ludhianvi from the film *Daag*:

> *Izzatain shohratain chahatain ulfatain*
> *Koi bhi cheez duniya main rahti nahi*
> *Aaj main hoon jahan kal koi aur tha ... aaj main hoon jahan kal koi aur tha*
> *Yeh bhi ek daur hai woh bhi ek daur tha...*

But presently, it is Aamir who rules the hearts of everyone in this world with his own rules.

AT HOME

THE FAMILY MAN

'I feel very blessed to have people in my family who are such lovely human beings. They are sensible, sensitive, caring, loving and reliable.'

Spending quality time at home with his mother Zeenat Hussain (left) and wife Kiran (right).

Facing page: A face that hides a million tales within.

Women have always been an integral part of Aamir's life. He sincerely believes in women empowerment. The actor has always drawn strength from the women he admires the most. The three most important women of Aamir's life are his mother Zeenat, his ex-wife Reena and his present wife Kiran. He talks straight from the heart whenever it comes to these three ladies. Together they have shaped his personality. They have never allowed him to harbour any chauvinism. A conscientious heart and a sensitive nature are the qualities that constitute the character of this much-loved man who has a huge female fan following.

At a personal as well as a professional level, Aamir Khan has always been admired for his sensibility. To a large extent the credit for this goes to his mother who has shaped his disposition, while his father has influenced his life in a big way. 'My father's strong will and high

Left: Aamir's son Azad Rao Khan with his dearest mummy Kiran.

Centre: Aamir's daughter Ira (on the phone) after a football match with family and friends.

integrity has been inspirational,' Aamir expressed. He considers his father a true fighter, who did not give up despite all odds. 'My sensibilities might be different, but I have inherited some of his genes,' elaborated Aamir. He is also credited for bringing change in the way men look at women through some of the episodes of his famous television chat show *Satyamev Jayate* that dealt with marriage, dowry and female foeticide among many other issues. While his stardom is apparent, it shines through when he shows his natural self and reaches out to the people. Besides his family he credits his cousin Nuzhat, who had a profound influence on him, to condition his mind about the plight of women. 'She made me read Simone de Beauvoir's *Second Sex* when I was just 14 years old,' he told *Femina* magazine. She was the one who introduced him to fresh concepts in art, music, politics, and explained to him the finer nuances of human relationships.

Today, worldwide, Aamir Khan—the actor-producer-director—is considered a huge public figure with honest values. But this renowned personality has much more to him than what is generally known to people. He has always kept his professional life separate from his personal life by trying to maintain a fine balance, which is hard to keep when someone is as popular as him. While he has been able to keep an impeccable public persona, it has definitely led to curiosity about his personal life, which he guards quite fiercely. Growing up in a cosmopolitan Hindi film industry's Muslim family, this talented star has imbibed a more tolerant view towards life under the full glare of the media. He does manage to keep his private moments much to himself. For instance, till he and his second wife Kiran announced the birth of their first child, no one knew about it. They successfully managed to guard the information from leaking out beforehand to anyone. He certainly knows how to keep his family life under wraps unless he is ready to share a slice of it. But once he breaks any news relating to his personal life, he gets full media attention; such is the power of Aamir Khan. Like in the case of his widely-reported Haj pilgrimage with his mother. It was photographed all the way from the Mumbai airport to his sharing a meal with Pakistani cricketer Shahid Afridi.

Aamir with his uncle and mentor, Nasir Hussain.

Aamir's liberal upbringing in the city of Mumbai gave him an independent streak. He grew up with friends belonging to different religions in his neighbourhood. No wonder when he decided to marry his childhood sweetheart Reena Dutta, he did not think about the religious disparity between them. They shared an affinity for each other and as a young couple in love they did what their hearts told them to do. The initial opposition gave way to maturity and understanding shared by the two families. At the young age of twenty-one, Aamir married the nineteen-year old Reena on 18 April 1986. This was when he was starting off in the film industry. For the sake of the careers of all those who

At a press conference for Satyamev Jayate.

were associated with his first film *QSQT*, Aamir had to keep his marriage to Reena a secret for some time, but broke the news with utmost pride to the media when the film was declared a super hit. Even in his younger days, his decision of marrying Reena proved that he had a mature head. From this marriage, he got two beautiful kids Junaid (his eldest son) and Ira (his only daughter).

The media linked him with almost all his leading ladies. Though stories of his affairs with his beautiful co-stars were doing generous rounds in the media, he never let the gossip affect his married life. Aamir did not allow anyone to trespass on his privacy even though he has well accepted the virtues of being a public figure. According to him, it is his public image that everyone has the right to know about and not his private life; and he likes it that way. Thus, when the actor realised that gossip was an occupational hazard he dealt with it in the most practical fashion. He stopped talking to many media persons who approached him with regular stories of his 'affairs'.

Reena, who was earlier working in a travel agency, took a shot at production when Aamir asked her to take over the reins as

Left: Aamir, Reena and Jaya Bachchan sharing a joke among themselves.

Right: The first and only Filmfare *award trophy that Aamir accepted in the 'Best Male Debut' category for* Qayamat Se Qayamat Tak.

a producer of his ambitious venture *Lagaan*. The two grew up together and survived several troughs and crests in their lives. It was a love story that stood rock solid for nearly sixteen years. They ended their marriage in December 2002 with mutual consent. So, what happened between the two that made them fall apart? Both have been reticent about it till date. No one seems to be privy to his or her heartaches and sorrows. Both Reena and Aamir have not shared with anyone the issues that broke them as a couple. There was no bickering, no spate of ugly attacks and no filth that was splashed. Without washing their dirty linen in public, they were divorced. The two still share a healthy relationship, which is linked to their children. For the first time when Aamir finally spoke about their separation in media, he said, 'Probably the most traumatic period has been my divorce—not just for me but for everybody involved, I imagine. I can't think of any other significant low.' He confessed that he was in depression for three years, had stopped working and didn't even step out of the house. He spoke about this while interacting with leading ladies of Star Plus in a special show. They are still seen together in times of happiness and sorrow. 'I really value the 16 years Reena and I spent together. I have the highest respect and love for her. I will always have that,'

he told *Hindustan Times*. 'She has immense strength of character and patience. She is a valuable part of my life. Our relationship may have altered, but nothing and no one can take away what we have shared,' he said in an interview to *Femina* magazine in 2013.

A private moment—Aamir lovingly puts on earrings for his wife Kiran.

Being a private person that Aamir is, in all these years he allowed only very few people to get a glimpse of what the actor's private life is all about. Only recently, the actor had expressed his views on marriage when he was hosting one of the episodes of *Satyamev Jayate*. He addressed the youth in his column in *Hindustan Times* saying aptly, 'Let's give marriage the importance it deserves—in every sense, financial, emotional, mental ... Marriage is a terribly important part of life. It's a partnership you form, a companion you choose, hopefully for the rest of your life.'

Four years after his divorce with Reena, on 28 December 2005, Aamir married Kiran Rao, who had been an assistant to director Ashutosh Gowariker during the making of *Lagaan*. The marriage was registered under Special Marriage Act in Mumbai. He did not speak about their relationship in the media for at least a year and a half, during which they were in a live-in relationship. Once he was ready to announce it to the world, he did so. However, when Aamir decided to marry Kiran, there were a lot of speculations—nobody believed that such a big star will marry someone who was still working towards establishing her name in this industry.

They married with the full family in attendance in his farmhouse in Panchgani.

As a fourteen-year-old Kiran had seen *QSQT* on the new VCR her family had bought. She revealed, 'I loved him in it but I enjoyed the film more. I was like "What a great film, what great music, what acting and what a cute guy!"' What she might have never imagined was that years later she would marry this 'cute guy'. Before she got to know him closely, the only impression she had of him was 'he is one of the few good actors in the industry'. She added, 'Even the fact that he is a perfectionist and all; I genuinely didn't know any of this, until I met him and got to know him.'

So when Kiran received an offer to work with Aamir Khan's production house, she got pretty intrigued by the idea of being a part of his film though she knew that she would hardly interact with him. Her first encounter with him was on the bus in which they were travelling to Bhuj for a recce. Though no one imagined Aamir's company on that journey as the bus was full of technicians and crew members, 'Aamir Khan, who is a superstar, was also on the bus,' Kiran informed later. 'But Aamir was not just on the bus, he also made conversation with every assistant, asked their names, introduced himself,' she added. This first encounter with Aamir made Kiran realise that he was a regular chilled out person with no starry tantrums. 'He had no "filmi" persona about him at all,' she revealed. Though he was surrounded by security guards, she found him completely down to earth. She felt there was no snobbery or "I don't talk to assistants" kind of attitude in him, which impressed her.

Exchanging greetings with Mukesh Ambani at a public function.

Aamir remembered their word-building games, which they used to play on the sets of *Lagaan*. His general impression about her was of a really nice, warm, happy, bright girl who is fun to be with. He also confessed that the earrings which the character Bhuvan wore in *Lagaan* actually belonged to Kiran, which he borrowed from her. After that they met while Kiran was doing

Aamir and Kiran surrounded by security guards on their way to watch a special preview of Taalash.

some work on the Goa schedule of *Dil Chahta Hai*. That is when she reminded him that he owed her a pair of earrings in exchange for the ones he borrowed for *Lagaan*. Aamir actually went with Reena, his wife at that time, and shopped for earrings from the Taj hotel shop for Kiran.

However, he actually got to know her better much later, when they were shooting a commercial for Coke. As Aamir was also producing it, they happened to spend much more time together. By that time he was single once again and they started dating on and off. Both of them, at that time, were not keen on a long-term relationship. But after a few months of spending time with him, Kiran started falling in love with Aamir, though she did not expect

Below: Aamir with co-stars Saif Ali Khan and Akshaye Khanna in Dil Chahta Hai.

anything serious to come out of such a casual relationship. She confessed, 'I felt like "Oh ... this is someone I really want to spend more time with and this is someone I want to know better." But I fell in love with him quite early ... a couple of months spending time intimately with him, I was hooked.'

During those days, after splitting up with Reena, Aamir was raw and damaged. 'Emotionally, I was very brittle at that point of time,' Aamir accepted. He was not ready to get into a committed relationship. However, it was not easy for him to treat his relationship with Kiran as just a casual one. 'Slowly I felt that when I am with her, I am comfortable and happy and open to share anything with her. Actually, we were friends first and then lovers. I felt relaxed after years,' he added. So what made Aamir realise that she was special? It was when, once while feeling very low, Kiran called him. The call went on for half an hour and when he put the phone down he found himself gravitating towards her. When he confessed his feelings about her to his sister Nuzhat, she advised him to stay away from Kiran, as he was too damaged at that time to take it forward. But Aamir could not control his heart and took their relationship a step further by asking her to move in with him.

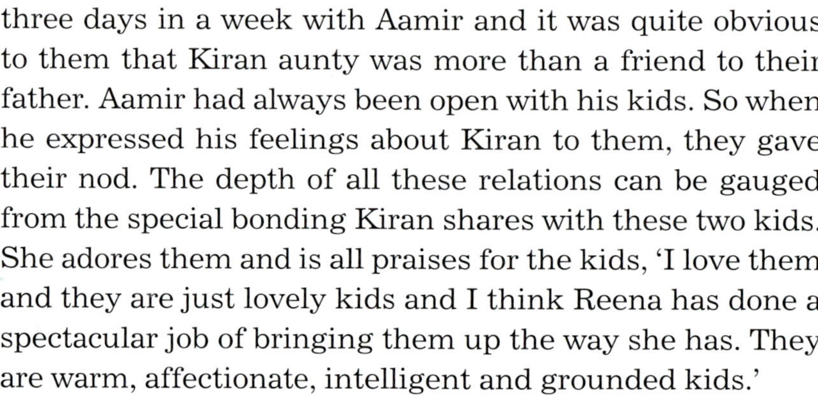

As his children have always been his first priority, it was important for Aamir to take them into confidence before he started living with Kiran. After his separation with Reena, the kids were spending three days in a week with Aamir and it was quite obvious to them that Kiran aunty was more than a friend to their father. Aamir had always been open with his kids. So when he expressed his feelings about Kiran to them, they gave their nod. The depth of all these relations can be gauged from the special bonding Kiran shares with these two kids. She adores them and is all praises for the kids, 'I love them and they are just lovely kids and I think Reena has done a spectacular job of bringing them up the way she has. They are warm, affectionate, intelligent and grounded kids.'

Aamir and Kiran attending the wedding of nephew Imran Khan with Avantika Malik.

After spending some quality time together they mutually agreed to get married. Kiran believes that they married more to keep people at large, happy. 'We were quite happy being together,' she explained. Now Aamir is happily married to someone who shares his passion for making films. Kiran fondly calls him *Chhotte*. Their relationship experienced several magical moments, one of them was the candlelight dinner they had in Panchgani. 'While I was working on *Taare Zameen Par*, I convinced her to go out for dinner with me in Panchgani. We drove towards Mahabaleshwar and stopped somewhere in the middle of the wilderness for a candlelight dinner,' said Aamir in an interview to *The Week*. Kiran confessed in the same interview, 'I might forget everything in my life but it is quite impossible to forget that evening.'

Aamir shares what he loves about Kiran. 'I love her energy; it's a very vibrant and positive energy which I find comforting and healing. She is a very happy person.' Kiran is extremely protective of Aamir and can pick up a fight with anyone who upsets him. However she fascinates Aamir with her knowledge about art, music and many more things. Aamir also likes her sense of aesthetics and design, and is totally in love with her creative instinct. Aamir's sensitivity never fails to touch Kiran's heart; she finds this quality of his very endearing. He makes a lot of fun of her that actually amuses Kiran; makes her laugh a lot and always keeps her on toes. When Kiran was asked to describe her husband in two words, she said, 'A good human being and hugely talented at the same time.'

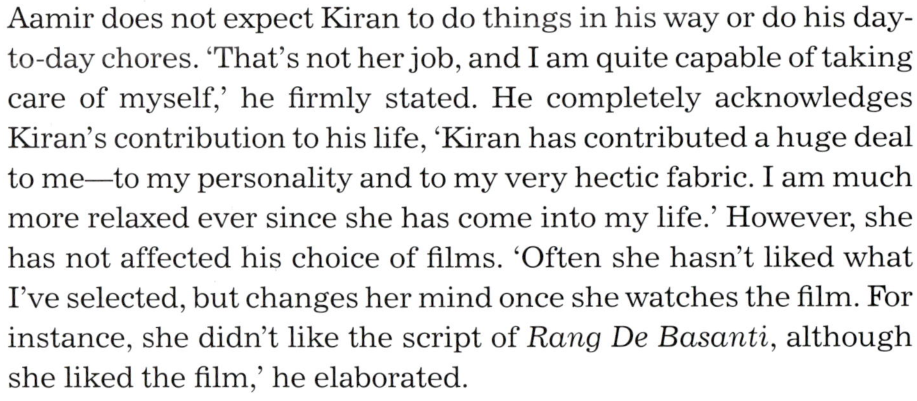

Aamir does not expect Kiran to do things in his way or do his day-to-day chores. 'That's not her job, and I am quite capable of taking care of myself,' he firmly stated. He completely acknowledges Kiran's contribution to his life, 'Kiran has contributed a huge deal to me—to my personality and to my very hectic fabric. I am much more relaxed ever since she has come into my life.' However, she has not affected his choice of films. 'Often she hasn't liked what I've selected, but changes her mind once she watches the film. For instance, she didn't like the script of *Rang De Basanti*, although she liked the film,' he elaborated.

Aamir reliving the Andaz Apna Apna *days with Salman Khan on the sets of* 10 Ka Dum.

While there are several qualities which this couple admires in each other, there are certain habits of each other which annoy them as well. Like Aamir's reading habit annoys Kiran, owing to which Aamir doesn't indulge much into meaningful discussions with her. The talkative nature of Kiran is something that bugs Aamir the most as it intrudes into the time he loves to spend with his books. Like most regular couples, if Aamir is boss on the sets, Kiran is at home but she always consults him while taking big decisions, primarily to avoid the chances of him complaining about it later.

Aamir, Kiran and Azad on their way to Mumbai airport.

On reflection, 2012 has turned out to be a remarkable year for Aamir. Kiran and Aamir are now proud parents of a child whom they named Azad Rao Khan. He was born to a surrogate mother using the IVR (in-vitro fertilisation) method on 1 December 2011. Aamir told *People* magazine, 'Just his birth and having him around is the best thing to have happened to us.' He told *Femina* that Azad is a fantastic kid, who is very quick and very communicative. Aamir revealed that until the time Azad was born, Kiran's entire focus was on Aamir. 'Now I have to share her attention with Azad and I am happy to do that,' he cheerfully added.

People close to the actor say that he has changed a lot after the birth of his son Azad. He has not only become much more outgoing but has also stopped taking himself too seriously. With Azad, Aamir is rediscovering himself every day. He is thoroughly enjoying this phase of his life. 'Azad is Aamir's spitting image. His son has made Aamir far more gregarious and fun-loving and the actor is now reaching out to many more people than ever before,' told a friend of his to *Mumbai Mirror*.

Earlier, owing to his busy schedule Aamir was not able to spend much time with Azad, but now he plans his schedule in such a way that he gets to spend at least half an hour every morning with him. Kiran is the one who is playing the role of a hands-on parent to Azad. 'She is enjoying motherhood and that's what she wants to do. Once in a while I do try and give her a break but she brushes it aside,' laughs Aamir.

If Azad is Aamir's weakness, in a positive sense, Junaid and Ira are his strengths. Though the custody of both the children is with Reena, Aamir is still an active father to them. From time to time he can be seen with Reena and their children enjoying dinner dates. 'I am always anxious about my children's well being, and often helplessly torn by worry,' he confessed. But now he is learning the art of 'easing off' from his daughter who keeps instructing him to chill. But Aamir still has a hard time putting her teachings into practice. The twenty-one-year-old Junaid is now assisting

director Rajkumar Hirani in the next Aamir starrer, *P.K.* On this Aamir said, 'It was my suggestion that Junaid learns something about cinema. I am looking forward to working with Junaid in *P.K.* I don't know what his future plans are. This is his first experience in films. I just hope he finds this experience exciting, enriching and a pleasant one.'

Seems like, life has come a full circle for the actor as he now sees his son too moving on the same lines. He truly wishes that Junaid make his career in films but would support him in whatever other choice he makes. His daughter Ira is still in the stage of completing her basic education. Though most of Aamir's education has not been formal, he truly acknowledges the significance of education but not in the formal sense of the word. More than formal education, he insists on the significance of acquiring knowledge. 'Gathering knowledge and experience, and getting that understanding is very important,' he asserted. He feels it is too early to talk about

The silver jubilee party of Qayamat Se Qayamat Tak. *L to R: Aamir's elder son Junaid; brother Faisal; former wife Reena; Avantika Malik, Imran Khan; daughter Ira, Aamir Khan, Kiran Rao, Nuzhat, Mansoor Khan with other family members.*

Aamir in a discussion with the staff at his office including wife Kiran.

Ira's career plans but is completely okay if she chooses to make her career in films. 'If it's good enough for me, it's good enough for her,' he asserted.

Another characteristic of Aamir that stands out in his character is his level of commitment towards his family and friends. Whether in his professional or personal life, he never forgets to keep his promises. Long back, he promised to take his mother for Haj. Despite being extremely busy with his professional commitments, quite the family man that Aamir Khan is, he recently accompanied his mother, Zeenat Hussain, on a pilgrimage to Mecca. After returning from the hectic Chicago schedule of *Dhoom: 3* and attending the music launch of *Talaash*, he somehow managed to squeeze in this trip. Like a dutiful son, he embarked on a fourteen-day holy trip to Mecca with his mom, eight other family members and a Maulana. Aamir left no stone unturned to make this Haj pilgrimage a memorable one for everybody. The group stayed at

Hotel Al Massa in Mecca and Hotel Elaf Taiba in Medina; both four-star hotels that are at a walking distance from the holy spots and are known to cater to the most discerning of international travellers.

Aamir greeting Amitabh Bachchan and child prodigy Kautilya Pandit from Haryana on the sets of Kaun Banega Crorepati (KBC) *during the shoot of a Children's Day special episode.*

This was his first Haj trip. 'It was a moving and spiritually overawing experience. A very emotional and introspective moment for me. At the same time, I felt very close to God,' shared Aamir. He summarised his experience, 'The character and beauty of the place has a surreal feeling. Especially when you go to the Maidan (ground) of Arafat—that's the most important moment of the trip ... A sense of catharsis overtook me.' He now finds himself at peace, 'Yes, I am much happier and at peace than I used to be. I pray that all Muslims who intend to go for the Haj should make their trip unfailingly.' Though he is a Haji now but to him it's not important how people address him but how he feels within, 'I have become more spiritual than I ever was ... I certainly want to lead a noble or good life where hopefully I won't commit mistakes like I have done in the past. I will try to live as honestly as I have lived in the past, without having to compromise with anything and without hurting anyone,' he added.

Aamir lives with Kiran in the same building in Bandra where he has spent his childhood. The smooth, spacious cream interiors of the house reflect the personality of this couple. Close to 2,000 books that adorn different parts of his house, including the kitchen, display his love for reading. Like his movies, his choice in books is eclectic—right from Urdu poetry to Shakespeare to autobiographies, as well as novellas. Aamir confirmed, 'My first instinct when I go home is to pick up a book, not the remote. I've been reading since I was six.' Besides books, his other interests are chess and cricket. 'I absolutely love cricket and chess. Not a single film has been ever shot where we have not had a cricket match between the cast and the crew.' He also has keen interest in PC games and music. From Bob Dylan to Sufi qawwali CDs, he enjoys them all.

Aamir's personal life does not only revolve round his immediate family; he shares close relationships with his cousins as well. Right from childhood they have all shared an unbroken bond of love. Aamir's relationship with his cousins is a poignant one. His cousin sister Nuzhat, who is a qualified clinical psychologist, has always been his sounding board since he was ten and she fifteen. 'She is one person I go to when I need to talk about anything,' he said warmly in an interview to *India Today*. 'She is a great thinker,' he added. She is also the one Aamir confided in when he first fell in love. Nuzhat highly admires Aamir's level of professionalism. She likes the fact that her brother always gives due respect to everyone in his personal as well as professional life. She believes that Aamir is fastidious about his honesty and simply cannot tell a lie. 'But he is not superhuman. He does make mistakes. He hurts himself. But he is totally open to learning and feeling new things, which I think is an act of courage,' she said. Even though his elder cousin Mansoor is not around most of the time, he is also a strong chain in this link. The other two people, whom he is really close to, beside his family and relatives, are Satyajit Bhatkal, who directed *Satyamev Jayate* (and also a documentary on the making of *Lagaan*) and Amin Hajee, the guy who played the mute character Bagha in *Lagaan*.

Khan essentially remains a middle-class man. He needs his family round him. He proudly admits to reading Bollywood trade papers. As a child, his father would make him write down the box-office collections of his films on the phone from places such as Amravati and Aurangabad. The knowledge which he gained then comes in handy now. Though Aamir does not open up to just anybody, he cherishes his relationships. Be it his family, friends or simply his make-up man for more than ten years, Jogi, or his man Friday, Sunil, he treats everyone with utmost respect and gets the same in return. The man who does not carry his cell phone on him, travels in a Land Cruiser, is always followed by an entourage comprising of policemen, private security personnel and his

Aamir interacts with the audience inside the auditorium after the promo launch of Dhoom: 3.

Facing page: A special photo shoot for Ghulam *at 6:30 in the morning.*

other private personnel. Kiran sometimes accompanies him, but mostly prefers to travel in her steely silver BMW 5 Series.

For Aamir, people often use the term 'perfection' but it has never been his intention. The actor has always been driven by passion. When it comes to his life in this film industry, he believes that it can be well symbolised through his favourite song sung by Mukesh:

> *'O re taal mile nadi ke jal mein*
> *Nadi mile saagar mein*
> *Saagar mile kaun se jal mein*
> *Koi jane na...'*

On the personal front he considers himself a simple person. Irrespective of what Aamir thinks of himself, to us he is much more than a simple man. Today, Aamir needs no crutch, no other inanity to declare his brand equity. As of now he elevates himself much above his contemporaries as a game changer from time to time.

THE COMMON SENSE OF BEING AAMIR KHAN

by Mayank Shekhar

'I am not an activist. I am an entertainer. I know that is my primary function. But I do have a degree of sensitivity to certain issues, and like any other person I would also like to make a positive impact on our society by speaking out whenever I feel the need to.'

Driving back from the launch of Kiran Nagarkar's book *God's Little Soldier* in New Delhi, Aamir Khan happened to be stuck in a traffic jam on the road that goes through Jantar Mantar. The astronomical observatory off Connaught Place is an open-air tourist destination that usually doubles up as venue for mass public protests. That day, on one side of the road were activists of the Narmada Bachao Andolan (NBA) asking for rehabilitation of villagers who would lose their land once the height of the Sardar Sarovar Dam got raised. On the other side of the same road were people demanding long overdue relief for the Bhopal Gas tragedy's victims.

Facing page: Aamir in a still from Dhoom: 3

Serenading his love with the song 'Chand sifaarish' *from* Fanaa.

Facing page: Aamir with friend Prasoon Joshi interacting with the media at press meet for Satyamev Jayate.

Aamir asked to be briefed on the issues of the day in his car. Satisfied with the urgency of both appeals, he got out, almost on impulse, he suggests, and sat with the two groups at Jantar Mantar. The day got selectively reported. Only his endorsement of NBA's protest got widely publicised. Gujarat's Youth Congress burnt the actor's posters. So did the Bharatiya Janta Party, which was safely in power then. It has remained in power in Gujarat for years now. The Chief Minister Narendra Modi ordered a ban against Aamir's latest film *Fanaa* in his state. This was a strange personal attack that went largely unchallenged. Speaking up for a cause is a citizen's natural right in a democracy. Celebrities are soft targets. They have a lot more to lose. There was immediate financial loss for Aamir's film. He never submitted an apology.

This was in 2006. It's not hard to tell why the state of Gujarat should've gone after an actor's endorsement of a demand that after all merely echoed the ruling of the nation's Supreme Court. The issue was broadly political. The state has reasons to fear Bollywood stars. They command greater attention and crowds than most seasoned politicians at pre-election rallies do. They're certainly more loved than politicians. They're likely to be heard more. Aamir adds to this natural charisma a rare touch of credibility. He's mindful of this image. The political party in question would have known this. They had to act fast, blow things out of proportion and divert attention swiftly. They succeeded. Realpolitik, in the short run, usually wins.

In 2003, when Coca-Cola was facing flak from a non-governmental agency for pesticide and insecticide content in their drinks, the company chose Aamir over a detailed advertisement to clarify their stand. The actor certified on public television the safety levels of the drink he endorsed. He suggests he could have cancelled his advertising contract over the same issue, become a national hero overnight, fighting for public health against a multinational giant. But he didn't. Without the company's knowledge, he had all claims of the Coca-Cola company first independently verified by his lawyers through a neutral laboratory. Once convinced, he spoke the truth. His argument was simple enough to have escaped the general public: 'It's not that pesticides and insecticides are added to manufacture Coke. They already exist in water that is used for agriculture. Given that the same water goes through five levels of

treatment for the manufacture of Coke, if anything, there are considerably less pesticides in cola than there are in the water we drink, and because of it, the foods we consume.'

About a decade later, the actor had cancelled all his product endorsement contracts anyway, which would have hit his annual salary by about Rs 100 odd crores or so. He was producing and anchoring a television show that would take up a new social issue every Sunday. It wouldn't have been morally correct to be seen peddling products on the side through advertising, while professing social causes between the commercial breaks. He understood this. The show raised close to Rs 100 crore from the public toward chosen charities featured in its episodes instead.

Six years since his first public tryst with a social cause, Aamir by now had a platform of his own to speak his mind as a citizen and a public figure. What he said, the nation at least heard, whether they followed or not is hard to verify. The governments of the day—whether at the Centre or the states—certainly took notice, and in many cases, even swung into action. Clearly this time politics didn't win. The intentions weren't questioned. The facts were measured. Every Sunday, the topics of national concern, trending on Twitter, would be on every Facebook update, and phone calls would fly across the country with people giving their own take on various social problems.

The journalists around me I realised resented the show *Satyamev Jayate* ('Truth Alone Prevails') the most. It reminded them of their own impotence. Most had probably joined their profession for the same missionary zeal the weekly programme stood for. Corporate profits and one eye on the eyeballs had made most of mainstream news media a redundant vehicle to address genuine, deeper, long-term public concerns. Scribes were best trained to execute shoot-and-scoot, '*aaj tak ki taaza khabar*' ('today's fresh news') kind of reporting. *Satyamev Jayate* was public affairs journalism at its best. And it came from a Bollywood star. The public acceptance must have also ensured healthy profits. Aamir was once again labelled a marketing guru.

Contrary to public perceptions, on my brief interactions with the actor over years, I haven't found Aamir to be a genius. I've noticed in his ticking mind instead a quality that usually eludes most geniuses, which is clarity of thought. It's striking. There are few people I know who can narrow down their understanding of an issue to a basic, rock-solid first-principle argument, which holds true for them, and which remains a strongly glued prism to see the world from. Surely he could take a while to carefully arrive at this world view. But he's not a muddled thinker. Once he takes a stand, he does stand up for it. He's no slim shady that way either.

Few months after the launch of his show, I interviewed him over the Anna Hazare anti-corruption movement that had fizzled out. He had actively campaigned for Hazare's team by lending his presence at the social activist's fast in Delhi. Aamir's answer was pointed: 'There is a law that says that if you're caught with embezzling public funds, you go to jail for six months. But it doesn't say that you have to return that money. Would you not want a law that states that you

Aamir visited Anna Hazare (centre) standing beside Manish Sisodia (left) at Ramlila Maidan, New Delhi to support the Jan Lokpal bill.

have to restore the stolen funds back to the public exchequer as well, yes or no?' Yes. I guess.

On the Narmada Bachao Andolan, Aamir said, 'Common sense still can't explain to me why they (politicians), who are supposed to be working for the people, should have an issue with rehabilitating people. Or that they should attack me instead for asking for it. I was only echoing what the Supreme Court had already said.'

The word 'common sense', you will notice, comes up quite often in conversation with the filmmaker. The word itself is a misnomer of sorts. In a world where common sense is so uncommon, Aamir is rightly considered a path-breaker. He applies the same first-principle rule to his films. This helps him repeatedly defy conventional market wisdom.

If I'm not mistaken three films on the revolutionary freedom fighter Bhagat Singh released in the same year 2002. They all bombed in theatres one after the other. Aamir's *Rang De Basanti* in 2006 was about the same era and the same set of freedom fighters. The film remains a landmark in Indian cinema. Apparently movies on serious issues, set in a village, or based on sports, don't work in Bollywood. *Lagaan* was both a sports film and also based on a village. *Taare Zameen Par* dealt with the crucial issues of dyslexia and child education system. *Peepli (Live)* was a rural film, plus on the serious issue of farmers' suicides. They are all now considered Bollywood entertainers in their own right. In fact the worst sufferer from market logic over serious issues is the entire business of journalism itself. *Satyamev Jayate* proved that great research-based journalism can deliver an interested, eager audience, and still be a commercial success.

So what does Aamir Khan know that others do not? That people respond to engaging stories, effectively told? This is no different from what everybody knows. What sets Aamir apart is he can tell a good story from a bad one, and pick the most effective ones to bring to life on screen—the size of that screen doesn't matter. It's a special talent. It can neither be mined by going through empirically determined commercial logic, or following strict diktats of genres that work. He is a voracious reader. This probably helps.

Mukesh Ambani (extreme left), Aamir Khan, Neeta Ambani and Sachin Tendulkar at the CNN-IBN Real Heroes Awards 2012.

More importantly, the honesty of his intent, even in a grotesquely madcap comedy *Delhi Belly*, shows. People respect his choices. They're willing to bet on him. He becomes the change we want to see in our films.

What about stardom? Is he the biggest we've had? That is subjective, of course, like the question of stardom itself. By the early 2000s, the prevailing market logic was, 'What you see is what sells [*Jo dikhta ha woh bikta hai*].' You saw the same heroes' billboards map the streets of all of post-liberalised India, selling everything, from films to face-whitening creams. In 2001, after *Lagaan* and *Dil Chahta Hai*, possibly at the peak of his career, Aamir altogether disappeared from films and public life in general. He came back in 2005. In that sense, he's not like the superstars we've always known.

Aamir takes a break by reclining on his couch.

I still feel the narcissism within him is deeper than most of his contemporaries. He's taken his public persona and work more seriously than others. His legacy will survive public memory for much longer. I can imagine an extensive Aamir Khan films' retrospective at a major world festival five decades from now. I'm not sure if this may be true for any of his competitors. And I'm still not sure if he thinks about these things too much. Most who find a deeper meaning to their lives don't.

The last time I met him for an interview, he was finding out ways in which a list of Indian organic farmers could be passed on to the television viewers he was with at the weekly phone-in show for the All India Radio. Between meetings with business associates and his chartered accountant, taking edit calls on the next episode of his show, and after sitting for an interview with me over two long breaks, Aamir finally parked himself in the couch at his Pali Hill apartment to chat with a doctor who'd come over from Rajasthan, suggesting ways of making generic drugs easily available to the public. This is before the actor headed off for a costume trial for his next film *Dhoom: 3*! All in a day's work. You could tell a media professional vastly expanding the role of a movie star. This is rare. That way, yeah, he is rare…

Mayank Shekhar is a well-known film critic and writer.

SATYAMEV JAYATE

A LOVE LETTER TO INDIA

'This show is dear to my heart. I believe we need such shows to address and eradicate issues, which are usually swept under the carpet, in our society.'

Aamir Khan and Uday Shankar, CEO, Star India, at a press conference held in Mumbai regarding Aamir's first TV show.

Facing page: Observing carefully and mysteriously smiling to himself.

Is it possible for a movie star to affect the behaviour of 1.2 billion people? In a cinema-obsessed nation like India, the answer may well be yes. Popular movie stars over the years have strongly influenced the mindset of cinema lovers in India. If used sincerely, this influence can bring positive changes in the society. Today when most celebrities are viewed with suspicion, it is even more imperative that actors use their popularity and authority for a good cause. There is one actor who has realised this need and acted upon it. He is Aamir Khan.

The reach of Indian television is undeniable; it has the power to reach the masses. In fact, it has the ability to reach areas and regions where the 70mm screen is still an escapist dream. Aamir truly understands this power of Indian television. Thus, when Uday Shankar, CEO, Star TV asked him what he would like to do for television it set him thinking. The one thing he was sure of was that he wanted to utilise this powerful medium more effectively than others did. He said in an interview, 'I started thinking and a basic picture emerged.' With his trusted friend Satyajit Bhatkal, who had directed the *Lagaan* documentary *Chale Chalo,* they started exploring themes. For the two years that he was off films, Aamir plunged into the heart of India. Along with a compact team, he researched, discovered and met people spanning all states. Thus, when the idea of *Satyamev Jayate* ('Truth Alone Prevails') was officially presented to the channel it was met with an instant approval.

Television propelled him to a new high and provided him with an opportunity to undertake his role as a unifier a step further. Through his groundbreaking television show, Aamir attempted to live up to his ideals by indulging his conscience. This noble initiative of his for the betterment of society has made Aamir India's first superstar-activist.

Large hoardings advertising the show screamed '*Jab dil pe lagegi, toh baat banegi*'. It projected a new Aamir—Aamir the activist. What a sea change this was from the first-ever billboard that introduced Aamir as the boy next door in 1989 in the hoardings of *Qayamat Se Qayamat Tak*! At the programme's launch, Aamir stated, 'This show is an important step in my life and dear to my heart. It's been my most ambitious project by far.' He quoted to a reporter at the press conference, '*Satyamev Jayate* is my love letter to India. Even in the song, I refer to my country as a person. The show is all about my love for my country.' Aamir is an impressionable person. Though his continued association with CRY (Child Relief and You) and his efforts in the field of child education are lesser known, in *Satyamev Jayate* his humanitarian qualities were well reflected. The fact that he had lent aid to the victims of a flood in Ladakh, where some parts of *3 Idiots* had been shot, is another instance that talks highly about the sensitivity he has for people of India.

Aamir promoting his film at a theatre; film critic and trade analyst, Taran Adarsh (left), is seated next to him.

His show cast a spotlight on some of India's ugliest social problems—female foeticides, sexual abuse of children, honour killings, dowry, domestic violence, medical malpractice, insensitivity towards the physically disabled, pesticide poisoning, alcoholism, untouchability, plight of senior citizens, water crisis, terrible inequities of the caste system and so on. Though many of these are largely considered as women's issues, Aamir thinks differently, 'Let's face it, the problem lies with men. Women suffer because men take away their right to choose: the right to choose the way they want to live, love and dream.' He believes that this patriarchal mindset is hindering the nation's growth. He is sad to realise that a lot of women also buy into this patriarchal thinking and endorse it! Owing to this, the cycle continues. As the creator, producer and host of the show Aamir left no stone unturned and also invested his star power and credibility into the show to sensitise people about these issues. These were matters that we all knew existed in our society but we never wanted to admit it. Aamir demanded people to take notice and voice their objection against these harsh realities. This courageous move by Aamir had the potential to jeopardise his status as the beloved idol of millions but he had a bigger goal in mind—the upliftment of Indian society. Writer-director Rajkumar Hirani said that Aamir was betting that people who come to him for entertainment would also follow him on more serious topics. Commenting on the show, actor Salman Khan said, 'I have seen *Satyamev Jayate*. A good man doing a good deed. No ambitions. It's not that this has not been attempted by people before. But no one noticed it. But when Aamir picks up these issues, people take them seriously.'

Satyajit Bhatkal, director of Aamir's TV show Satyamev Jayate, *was also the production executive in* Lagaan.

Aamir believes that the young generation of the country can bring about lot of changes. For him, though, entering the small screen was for a purpose way beyond popularity and fame. He wanted every individual to understand the different social problems that people in India face constantly without any redress. Was this concept new to the people? Well, not really. Other shows in the past too had taken up social causes and public demands. However, what made *Satyamev Jayate* unique was the way it was presented to the audience.

Laughing heartily with close friend Prasoon Joshi.

The programme was shot in a number of states including Kerala, Rajasthan, Delhi, Kashmir and Punjab. It was also among the few television programmes to have explored the North-Eastern part of our country. Even before the concept of the show was revealed to the audience, the hype round it had already gained momentum. Critics, people, media and television experts were already offering their views and quoting expectations. But what made this reality show stand out from the rest, was the fact that it was based on an eagerness to provide solutions to some of our society's nagging and most serious problems.

Aamir did this show on his own terms and conditions. Although the show was bankrolled by Star India, he made it a point that it was simultaneously broadcasted by the state-owned terrestrial stations of the national telecaster Doordarshan. The show was shot in Hindi and dubbed in several Indian languages with subtitles in English to increase its reach. Known as a risk-taker and doing what he believes in, he aired his show on Sunday mornings at 11 am, though no one was sure if Indians would tune in on a holiday on Sunday morning to be hectored for ninety minutes on subjects they had previously chosen to sweep under their carpets. He did not want to just shock and shake people but wanted them to invest their time to discuss the issues that were purposely overlooked in society.

Backed by statistics and case studies the show awakened the *aam janta* (general public) to the evils of the society. He did not sugar-coat the messages to suit the desires of his audience. *Satyamev Jayate* had shown what Aamir wanted people to see. Each episode explored a single issue from all possible angles. His intelligence was reflected in the fact that in his show he had carefully avoided easy scapegoats. Individual culprits were not his target, rather all those who were involved in the evils of the society. He encouraged collective responsibility in his show. He strongly believes that in a way we all are responsible for these evils if we have never done anything to fight them.

This thirteen episode programme opened one lazy Sunday morning on 6 May 2012 and jolted the viewers from their sleep. According to a high-profile survey, *Satyamev Jayate* was able to achieve a rating of 4.27. This also included Doordarshan ratings. In fact, the very first episode reached out to as many as 8.96 million viewers. Such was the telephonic traffic that around one lakh viewers tried calling from all over the country, but only about twelve people were eventually able to get through and be a part of the historic programme. The show was appreciated by the film industry, political leaders, social activists and the common people.

Aamir, the crusader, pointing towards the 'truth'.

But unlike other shows that depend on TRPs, *Satyamev Jayate* worked on the premise that it had touched the hearts of the people all over the country. It had also set the cat among the pigeons in some sectors where the concerns stuck out like sore wounds. More importantly, the show succeeded in bringing a change of attitude among diverse Indians. Many viewers confessed that they had previously ignored several social problems that were covered in these thirteen episodes. They agreed that the show rekindled their interest in these oft-avoided topics.

The impact of the show can be gauged from the various developments that took place after some episodes on particular

Aamir Khan at the press conference regarding his debut on the small screen as the anchor of a revolutionary talk show.

themes were aired. For instance, an episode on the sexual abuse of children compelled the Lok Sabha to pass a long-overdue bill to protect children from molestation, while a segment on the exploitation of low-caste Indians led to a meeting and discussion with the Prime Minister, Dr Manmohan Singh. Some state governments were shaken out of their seats when hard facts exploded in the face of their officials. Aamir's high-wattage advocacy not only impacted the high and mighty of society and politicos but also people at the grass-roots level. Such was the influence of that section on female foeticide on the chief of Budania village in the state of Rajasthan that he set the police on those families that sought gender-determination tests and abortions. Ultimately, the licences of six sonography centres in Jaipur were cancelled by the government and on suspecting the involvement of twenty-four others in female foeticide, notices were issued to them. As a producer Aamir stated, 'My job was to make a show I believe in and I am very happy with the efforts of my team.'

On 29 July 2012, the final episode of the first season of the show was aired. The calculations made had revealed some astonishing figures. The show had reached to an aggregate TV audience in excess of 500 million while many more millions heard it on radio, watched episodes online and followed the discussion in the newspapers. The reach was so extensive that it may not be possible for us to calculate the actual total benefit Aamir had brought with this show to the Indian society by enabling some real change.

Looking at his 45th birthday greetings surrounded by fans at his Bandra home.

On 1 May 2013, Aamir visited Satyamev Jayate Bhawan, a shelter home built by an NGO, Snehalaya Foundation, and spent the day interacting with the survivors of domestic violence and dowry harassment. He had inaugurated the home in January 2013.

In this entire time what was endearing is that the persona of the public idol was pushed to the background. The contacts that he had made were between one human and another human, one Indian to another. When he spoke to the people at times he laughed, at times he shared their sadness and cried with them. He got emotional when he connected to strangers from remote corners of the nation. He made some loyal friends too. His feelings towards them were, 'I might not be able to solve all your problems but I can hold your hand and hug you and make you feel better.' After all, it was the thought that counted in the end.

At a press conference in Film City, Mumbai celebrating the silver jubilee of Qayamat Se Qayamat Tak.

Whether you appreciate or criticise him, you just cannot deny the power with which he forced you to confront the unpalatable truths about the Indian society. When he brought them to the centre stage in his show, they naturally got much more attention from all strata of the society. With the show, the crusader's focus was not just on the classes or a certain part of society but on the whole nation. He could have chosen the simpler path of making a movie rather than taking up the challenge of making Indians dedicate their Sunday morning to an engaging, insightful yet gruelling talk show. But then he is a public figure with a difference!

Such was his faith in this show that he also donned the role of a columnist in *Hindustan Times*. For example, he wrote a piece on the sexual abuse of children, 'Our children observe us closely. If we want them to speak up, then we should ensure that we let them know that they will be believed. Yes, not just heard but believed.' He hit the nail on the head by questioning whether parents really did hear their children out. 'Are we really listening to our children? Are we even capable of listening to them?' he queried. Aamir explained that it is open communication and trust that work in cases of such nature.

Renowned writer Shobhaa De in her column 'Politically Incorrect' urged her readers to hand it to Aamir for attempting the near impossible task of getting television audience to watch him doing a *Bharat Pita*. She believed that with *Satyamev Jayate*, a show

Surrounded by books, Aamir loves to read and a wide range of subjects interest him.

devoid of any flimsy entertainment value, Aamir had attempted to change the viewing pattern of the fickle Indian audience. 'Aamir hoped to carve out a brand new slot for himself; a slot with virtually zero competition from others. To achieve his objective, Aamir didn't pick a game show—he hoped to become the game changer,' she elaborated.

Talking about the show, Uday Shankar, CEO, Star India said that *Satyamev Jayate* was about compelling stories that raised the bar for television programming and created a profound experience for our viewers.

Addressing a press meet just outside his Bandra home on the occasion of his 45th birthday.

Shailaja Bajpai in her column 'Telescope' wrote the real reason for which people watched *Satyamev Jayate*. Even though the programme was tearful and made us feel miserable, true human stories always appeal to all. She believed that we watched it because it was personal. 'It was about you, them, the person across the aisle,' she concluded for us.

On reading the recent issue of *Time* magazine, Hollywood star Tom Hanks had expressed his admiration for Aamir Khan. He said, 'I really admire the work that Aamir Khan is doing.' He stated that very few celebrities take the initiative of coming forward to change the nation. He believed that Aamir had done a remarkable job with the show. He also asked everyone to support Aamir in this noble cause. As Hanks knows that giving back to society is tough, he accolades Aamir who truly understands his influential power of being a celebrity. Aamir is one of those few artistes who believes in giving back to the people who shower love on him. He has used his power on people in an optimum way through his show and acted as a catalyst for change, which won him Hanks' support and appreciation.

The show had not only influenced the Indian population but positively impacted Aamir as well. For him the project was almost like seeing life at its closest quarters. Aamir expressed himself, 'This is my effort to connect India to the people of the country, and more importantly to connect to myself. I feel I know my country better now. For me this was life's most enriching experience. I learnt so much from people and it is just good to connect to the people.'

Satyamev Jayate was not merely a television show; it was a movement that swept the country over a span of thirteen weeks

and forced people to think. It has made every Indian stand up and take responsibility for the evils in his surroundings, and more importantly, pledge to make it a better place to live in.

The show has become a benchmark for regular television producers now. A non-soap opera producer, Aamir has brought a novel perspective to reality shows. His comparison to Oprah Winfrey is inadequate to explain the influence and impact of his radical work. There is much more to him. On one hand, *The Hindu* had extolled how the actor had united Indians by highlighting mutually-shared joys and sorrows. It is not hyperbolic to say that now cricket and Aamir Khan unite the nation. On the other hand, he had inadvertently stirred some lazy souls into action. In October 2012, Aamir and Uday Shankar were honoured by the National Commission for Scheduled Castes at a function for creating awareness against social discrimination through their show. Delhi's Chief Minister, Ms Sheila Dixit requested Uday Shankar to bring back the show to create more awareness among the people and encourage them to stand up against the evils as a team. This most influential TV show also bagged the prestigious CNN-IBN Indian of The Year—Special Achievement Award 2012—for its path-breaking initiative.

With Uday Shankar after announcing his ambitious forthcoming venture on television.

Facing page: Empathising with Anna Hazare's honest cause at the Ramlila Maidan.

Aamir plans to start working on the second season of *Satyamev Jayate* after completing work on Rajkumar Hirani's *P.K.* He stated, 'This show is dear to my heart. I believe we need such shows to address and eradicate issues, which are usually swept under the carpet, in our society.' His team has already begun research work for the next season.

He is not a Gandhian or a young Anna Hazare. Can he be christened as being a modern Mangal Pandey who has scratched the surface of a mutiny against the evils and ills of society in twenty-first century India—that is anybody's guess!

AN ODE TO EXCELLENCE

by Vikas Chandra Sinha

Prakash, the original Padukone, was the first Indian world champion in an individual sport. In 1980, he won what can be called the grand slam of badminton—the Danish and Swedish Opens, the All England Championship followed by the World Cup. He remained a top ten player in the world for almost ten years. Before him, India had known success in team sports—there were the talismanic hockey victories at the Olympics and the occasional cricket triumph but individual success on a world stage was sporadic—a lone Olympic bronze from K.D. Jadhav in 1952, the nearly there performance by Milkha Singh at the 1960 Olympics and Wilson Jones winning at the World Amateur Billiards Championship in 1958 and 1964.

Prakash Padukone occupies the highest pantheon in Indian sports but he is arguably the gentlest and the most down-to-earth icon that India has produced. His interview with Shekhar Gupta on NDTV's *Walk the Talk* was a pleasure to watch. It is worth quoting an exchange from the interview which reveals the character of the great man.

Shekhar: You knew this what they always called the Prakash ability, calling everybody probably the greatest, probably the second greatest and you keep yourself out of it.

Prakash: Compared to the people I mentioned, you know like Rudy (Hartono) has won the All England eight times, (Martin) Frost has reached the final eight times, won four and I have reached the finals only twice.

Facing page: Performing a hat trick during the merchandise launch for Dhoom: 3.

Shekhar: But you have carried with you a great degree of difficulty...

Prakash: No that is there, that is there. So, maybe compared to the Indians, and the facilities which were available, I think I have done well. But I don't consider myself world's great. Maybe considering the facilities, I have done my best.

But what has this got to do with Aamir Khan or films? Like Prakash, Aamir has been on the top of his profession for a long time, a part of the Khan troika that has ruled Hindi cinema for two decades now. Like Prakash, he is a quiet achiever—the battle for the so called numero uno position among Hindi film actors has played out in the media between Shahrukh Khan and Salman Khan. Aamir does not attend the numerous film award ceremonies that dot the annual calendar calling them meaningless recognition, a stand that would be suicidal for lesser stars. He is reputed to be more comfortable curling up with a book after a day's shoot rather than attend the many parties the film glitterati are expected to grace, again highly atypical behaviour for film stars who are expected to be seen and heard to reinforce their star image.

He may have stood aside in the race to being numero uno, but he has maintained a commanding position in the filmgoer's mind as 'Mr Perfectionist'. That is the reason why filmmakers keep returning to him with challenging projects in spite of his reputation as a difficult artiste to work with. This image is a testimony to the sustained commitment to excellence that Aamir has maintained for the last two decades. Barring some of his first few films, all his projects—whether commercially successful or not—have a certain quality about them. David Light summarised this quality in an article for the *Khaleej Times*, 'The anticipation surrounding an Aamir Khan film opening is quite unlike any other cinematic event Bollywood has to offer. When either of the other two Khans within the powerhouse triumvirate announces a new picture, mass hysteria is sure to ensue among their respective followers. However, with The Perfectionist's offerings, a more subtle excitement emerges, which not only transcends fans of particular genres, but unites cinemagoers across every societal boundary, such is the hallmark of excellence Aamir's productions evoke.'

Aamir Khan's association with a project is almost like a stamp of quality. The propensity to choose and work in projects of a certain quality puts Aamir one up on even the greatest actor-stars of Bollywood—Ashok Kumar, Dilip Kumar, Amitabh Bachchan—all of whom had their fair share of poor films. Given the culture of fanatical star worship in India, it surely must be very tempting for a superstar like Aamir to coast along on his star power. Therefore, it is refreshing to come across someone like Aamir who refuses to compromise on his own standards in his projects, always focussing on cinematic quality rather than charisma alone. Celebrities can often get away with shoddy work in their chosen fields by relying on their star status. This is more so in our country, a point that Prakash Padukone was subtly making in his interview with Shekhar Gupta, when he talked down his own achievements. In his mind, excellence has a certain absolute standard—irrespective of whether a star is being evaluated. Aamir constantly reminds us of this adage.

During a midnight shoot for Ghulam.

Aamir burst upon our consciousness with *Qayamat Se Qayamat Tak* in 1988 but followed it up with some mediocre offerings like *Love Love Love*, *Deewana Mujh Sa Nahin*, *Tum Mere Ho* and so on. *Dil* that released in 1990 proved to be a turning point for him and after that Aamir preferred to work on one movie at a time and chose his projects with great care. What followed were a string of movies that established his reputation as a purveyor of quality cinema—*Dil Hai Ke Manta Nahin* (1991), *Jo Jeeta Wohi Sikandar* (1992), *Hum Hain Rahi Pyar Ke* (1993), *Andaz Apna Apna* (1994), *Rangeela* (1995), *Raja Hindustani* (1996), *Ishq* (1997), *Ghulam* (1998), *Sarfarosh* (1999) and *Earth* (1999). Not all of these films were runaway hits but many of them have attained cult status. In fact, it is the quality of his failed films in the 1990s which ensured that the moniker 'Mr Perfectionist' sat lightly on Aamir's shoulders—films like *Daulat Ki Jung* (1992), *Isi Ka Naam Zindagi* (1992), *Parampara* (1992), *Baazi* (1995), *Akele Hum Akele Tum* (1995) and *Aatank Hi Aatank* (1995).

The critical and commercial failure of *Mann* (1999) and *Mela* (2000) led Aamir to do a rethink and embark on the most creative part of his career. He was always interested and involved in all the aspects of filmmaking in his projects, and in 2001 he turned producer with *Lagaan*. The story of a village cricket team set in the British Raj was unconventional to say the least, but the film turned out to be a cinematic milestone. There has been no looking back. A line of mesmeric films followed, with Aamir as actor, producer or director—*Dil Chahta Hai* (2001), *Mangal Pandey* (2005), *Rang De Basanti* (2006), *Fanaa* (2006), *Taare Zameen Par* (2007), *Ghajini* (2008), *Jaane Tu... Ya Jaane Na* (2008), *3 Idiots* (2009), *Peepli (Live)* (2010), *Delhi Belly* (2011), *Dhobi Ghat* (2011) and *Talaash*

Aamir with Sonali Bendre in the sensually romantic song 'Jo haal dil ka' *from* Sarfarosh.

(2012). These films have burnished his reputation for quality into the minds of every filmgoer in India. The post *Lagaan* phase of his career has been doubly satisfying for him. He has caught up and surpassed the other Khans in terms of box-office success. In *3 Idiots* and *Ghajini*, he has delivered mega-blockbusters to rival Salman's *Maine Pyar Kiya* and *Hum Aapke Hain Koun..!* and also Shahrukh's *Dilwale Dulhania Le Jayenge*. *Lagaan* and *3 Idiots* have caught the imagination of all Indians and are turning into timeless classics that will not only secure Aamir's place in cinematic history but will also be positioned in the rarefied league of films that have come to define Bollywood—films like *Mother India*, *Guide*, *Anand*, *Sholay*, *Deewar* to name a few.

In an industry where most actor-stars cultivate a set image, Aamir has defied categorisation. He has starred in a fairly eclectic mix of genres spanning romantic, action, comedy, suspense and anti-hero films. Rajeev Mantri zeroed in on this quality in an article on *The Wall Street Journal* website, 'Khan is consistently inconsistent in an industry known for formulaic fare. Like venture capitalists, who tend to think and invest in herds, film producers tend to go with "what works" at the box-office. Aamir Khan, as actor and more recently as producer and director, has broken new ground with every film, especially since the release of the Oscar-nominated *Lagaan* in 2001.' The breathtaking diversity in his films has spanned more than two decades and is perhaps matched only by the great 1970s thespian, Sanjeev Kumar's oeuvre. But unlike Sanjeev Kumar, Aamir has firmly remained a darling of the masses throughout his career. Among superstars, Rajesh Khanna during his dream run between 1969 and 1972, and Amitabh Bachchan in his meteoric rise to megastardom between 1975 and 1977, matched this creative versatility. But soon after, both became prisoners of their respective screen images. Aamir has been able to avoid this trap and cannot be accused of playing himself in any of his

At the mahurat *of an ABCL film starring Amitabh Bachchan, Aamir and Madhuri Dixit, to be directed by Indra Kumar (2nd from right) that later got shelved.*

Facing page: Director Indra Kumar played a significant role in Aamir's film career.

movies, unlike many of his illustrious contemporaries. Navneet Mundhra in an article in IBNLive.com aptly sums it up, 'What sets him apart from his contemporaries is the fact that he chose unconventional subjects, played radical characters and still managed to dish out commercially successful movies which are also regarded as classics.'

What explains Aamir's excellence—the quality of his films, the versatility in his roles and the ratio of box-office success—that has sustained over such a long time span? Many students of cinema swear by the auteur theory which holds that a film reflects the director's personal creative vision as if he/she were the primary author. They believe that auteur directors are able to exert artistic control over all aspects of filmmaking. Others have tried to analyse

With Mamta Kulkarni during the filming of Baazi.

cinema in the framework of viewer response—in their view great filmmakers understand their audience and are able to deliver what matters to them. Both the viewpoints are right but the balance between the two is what delivers great cinema. On one hand, if a filmmaker tries too hard to be an auteur, he/she may create masterpieces which nobody watches like many art-house films of the 1980s. On the other hand, if he/she is led by the nose by the audience—the result could be mindless blockbusters, something Bollywood is routinely accused of. Aamir Khan has got this alchemy right and this explains his stupendous success. *The Wall Street Journal* opined that 'Mr. Khan has mastered the balance between art and commerce, pleasing the critics and pulling in hordes of audiences at the same time.'

Aamir in the get-up of a mafia don from Bombay during the shooting of Aatank Hi Aatank.

Only the greatest filmmakers get the balance between art and commerce right. Rishi Kapoor, the much loved star of the 1970s and 1980s, and the son of legendary filmmaker Raj Kapoor, hit the nail on the head when he told *Time* magazine, 'It takes a genius like my father to find the balance between what people want to see and what you want to show them.' Aamir has the same genius—he is an actor with sensibilities of a filmmaker. He is more comparable to the great actor-filmmakers like V. Shantaram, Guru Dutt and Raj Kapoor than to the great actor-stars like Dilip Kumar and Amitabh Bachchan. He prefers to creatively interpret the whole film and not just restrict himself to his role. He exerts his influence over all aspects of the film—something that has also led to clashes with some of his directors. His supposed clash with old friend Amole Gupte who had conceived *Taare Zameen Par* was perhaps the most poignant and as the producer he ended up taking the directorial reins. His instincts were proved right in the end.

The Wall Street Journal compared filmmaking to entrepreneurship, 'The role of a film producer is analogous to that of a venture capitalist. Good producers, like smart venture capitalists, know that it's not just about writing a cheque and it's just not about big stars and quality music. In the same way, simply providing venture funding or throwing money at a start-up cannot ensure success, and it's not necessarily a great thing for entrepreneurs to have lots of work experience and domain expertise in their industry. The actors and the director, like entrepreneurs, work to bring the script and business plan to life.' Successful entrepreneurship involves three key elements—embracing a vision and choosing the right strategy, creating a team aligned to the entrepreneur's vision and strategy and finally, ensuring efficient execution. Aamir's approach is similar; he chooses scripts carefully, works with like-minded people and the teams he has worked with have been quite innovative in the way they have conceived and executed films.

Navneet Mundhra writes, 'The prominent force behind Aamir's success is (an) uncanny, and immaculate sense of the script.' Aamir is extremely fussy while choosing his scripts. He did not even spare his wife Kiran Rao, whose first film *Dhobi Ghat* he produced. She famously said, 'I had to fight with him to protect my script.' Aamir is reputed to have rejected many of the scripts he reviews but not before going through each script thoroughly. One such writer

A scene from the climax of the film Mela.

who was rejected by Aamir told Manu Joseph in *Open* magazine, 'I was nobody then, but Aamir spent a lot of time with me discussing the story. He had so many questions. So many doubts. "Would this work, would people find this convincing ... I know people and the people won't accept it". He didn't know me at all, but we went to the toilet together and we peed standing side by side, talking about the script. In the end he said "no".' But there is a method behind the madness. Aamir tells Manu Joseph, 'When I am choosing a script, I don't think of the audience. I think of myself. I have to love it. Then I think of the audience. I wonder how can we tell this story without boring anyone. I have one interest in a film. The message is not important to me. What is important is that I don't bore you. I know what you want is entertainment. The only responsibility of a film is to provide it.' And he defines entertainment as, 'anything that engages the mind, heart and conscience or attention.' He is on record saying, 'Not all my films have social messages ... I do films that touch my heart and move me.' This is Aamir's alchemy—the balance between art and commerce that very few can master.

Aamir is equally choosy about the team he works with. As is apparent, he is a man with many questions who gets very involved with his projects and 'not just as an actor' as he told *Firstpost*. He is not a Raj Kapoor style 'auteur' whose word is law on the sets nor is he a supremely gifted actor like Amitabh Bachchan who can deliver a powerhouse performance even when all round him have no clue about what is going on. He needs to constantly interact with his team to interpret his role, 'I follow the character. I don't have a character already etched in my mind. I don't work this way ... I love (the) organic way where the story is already in place and we all join in as characters contributing to the story and bringing it alive.' Inevitably, he strays into the work domain of other people on the sets. The stories of interference are many and the most famous involve Mahesh Bhatt and Ram Gopal Varma—directors who have some claim to being auteurs in their own right.

Aamir has mastered the art of innovation. 'Aamir is the big brand that can make little innovations go mainstream,' writes Mahesh Murthy in a *Wall Street Journal* blog. He continues, 'The trick is that he doesn't really do wildly innovative stuff. He picks stuff just slightly ahead of the curve – "zara sa hat ke", as they say in Bollywood – and he executes it really well, pushing the market a wee bit ahead each time. *Three Idiots* was a nice-ish take on a rather ordinary book that came out a while ago – not the first on college life, certainly. *Ghajini* was a well-done take on a murder mystery based on a 10-year old movie, *Memento*. *Taare Zameen Par* wasn't the first story by a long way focusing on a special child. In fact, just looking at things from an innovation point of view in moviemaking, my friends Anurag Kashyap and Shashanka Ghosh are probably the ones burning the shrubs and clearing the way. Aamir then drives down the path in his Prado. And that's all right, I think. Everybody has their roles to play in this ecosystem.' His marketing campaigns though have been extremely innovative and effective. In *3 Idiots* the main character

A shot from the film Dhobi Ghat, *the directorial debut of Kiran Rao.*

disappears midway through the film. Aamir did the disappearing act while promoting the movie and sent the media on a wild-goose 'Aamir' chase. He travelled in disguise leaving behind small gold medallions with 'AK' stamped on them for people he had stumped. These medallions acted as entry passes to the film's premiere. While launching the music of *Talaash*, he recreated Hotel Lido which plays an important role in the movie, including calling in all junior artistes so that the exact ambience of the movie could be experienced.

In business the personality of the entrepreneur plays a large part in success or failure—so too in filmmaking. Aamir's greatest gift is his curiosity, his power of observation. As he told Manu Joseph, 'I am very curious about people, their

With Amitabh Bachchan on the sets of KBC *during a Diwali special episode in 2000.*

mannerisms ... I am interested in people.' He is proud of his connect with the audience, what he calls 'instinct about my own people'. The other defining trait is simplicity. Manu Joseph continues, 'The fact that Aamir chooses his films carefully has created a perception that he is a cerebral actor, but there is also a surprising intellectual austerity in him which might be a gift in the world he occupies. His films are simple and accessible, not because he has made an artistic compromise; they are that way because he too is simple.' Like all gifted artists, there is narcissism about Aamir but it is not the narcissism of a star rather the narcissism of leaving behind a legacy of work. There is an insecurity that keeps him going. As a young man, he wanted to be a tennis star but had to give up as he could not keep up with the practice required. He learnt his lesson, quoted in *Firstpost*, 'But as an actor I thought I won't do that mistake of not practicing every day. I won't allow myself to fall short.' Passion for his work is accompanied by courage of conviction, reflected in his comments to Subroto Bagchi writing in *Forbes* magazine, 'Do what makes you happy, don't worry about being successful. Be courageous. Live life on your terms.'

Aamir's holistic approach to filmmaking—a simple but diligent style of acting, passion for his work and oodles of self-confidence—means that the film, and not he as the star, is at the centre of each of his projects. He is a superstar who is never larger than his films. This attribute was most visible when he created, produced and hosted the television series *Satyamev Jayate*—a cross between a chat show and serious journalism wherein some of the ugliest social problems of India were highlighted. Aamir lent enormous credibility to the show but the real stars were the invitees who laid bare some of our society's worst-kept secrets. Compare this with Amitabh Bachchan's magnificent turn as the host of the television game show, *Kaun Banega Crorepati*. The show itself is nothing special; it is Amitabh's commanding presence which makes India glued to it. In contrast, Aamir's has a plain and understated presence in *Satyamev Jayate*. The stories of the people he invites on the show are the real scene-stealers.

'What is the role of the entertainer?' Aamir rhetorically asks in Bobby Ghosh's article in *Time* magazine. He answers it himself, 'It's to bring grace to society, to affect the way people think, to make social fabric stronger.' This search for grace is Aamir's ode to excellence.

That brings us back to where we started, to Prakash Padukone—the embodiment of grace if there was one. Prakash shared the secrets of success in an article for *LiveMint*, 'The success I achieved as a player ... behind each match and every stroke was a lot of thought and practice. And this is also where you realise that you cannot do it alone. I have a lot of people who have worked with me tirelessly at the back-end ... Finally, it is not easy to put passion over money. But it is possible—what you must ask yourselves is whether you would really like to do it every day, can you be the best in the world while doing it and can you create a larger impact in this world with what you are setting out to do? And believe me, you will find that life is a lot more meaningful— the pursuit of excellence is not an easy path, but there is certainly lots of light at the end of this tunnel.' A sentiment that Aamir captured in his film *3 Idiots* where the character he played kept repeating, 'Pursue excellence and success will follow anyway.'

Thank you, Aamir for your unwavering search for excellence.

Vikas Chandra Sinha is an IIT and IIM alumnus who admires Aamir's dedication to his profession.

गूँज

ECHO

नदिया की स्वतन्त्र धार	***The free stream of the river***
कल कल निनाद है सहस्रधार	***With gentle musical sounds of a thousand streams***
बड़ा तीव्र वेग साहस अपार...	***Flows strongly in its pace, with infinite courage...***
भँवर बन उमड़ा जब	***When it became a wave***
उमड़ा जब घूमड़ा जब	***Rumbling with a tide now and an ebb then***
इक सोच समुचि हिला गया...	***A thought jolted us out of our senses...***
कर दीप्तिमान प्रदीप्तिमान	***Bright and illuminated,***
समाज तुझमें समा गया...	***All of eternity dissolved in you...***
सच्चाई की पतवार थाम	***Holding on to the oar of truth***
जब गूँज बन निर्झर बहा	***When like an echo of a cascading waterfall***
तेज दीप्त प्रवाह बेध	***Your well-lit flow pierced***
प्रशस्त राह दिखा गया...	***Leading to a definite path...***
तू शाखों की उत्तुंग पात	***You are like a lofty row of branches***
है उदीप्तिमान है शक्तिमान	***Luminous and Powerful***
समग्र समष्टि का अभिमान...	***The pride of the whole universe rests in you...***
रैना	*by Raina*

Facing page: A painting of Aamir by artist Rajesh Srivastava.

A
R.SRIVASTAV '13

FILMOGRAPHY

Year	Film	Role	Co-starring
2013	*Dhoom: 3*	Sahir	Katrina Kaif, Abhishek Bachchan, Uday Chopra, Tabrett Bethell, Jackie Shroff
2012	*Talaash: The Answer Lies Within*	Inspector Surjan Singh Shekhawat	Kareena Kapoor, Rani Mukerji (Mukherjee), Nawazuddin Siddiqui, Raj Kumar Yadav
2011	*Dhobi Ghat (Mumbai Diaries)*	Arun	Kriti Malhotra, Monica Dogra, Prateik Babbar
2009	*3 Idiots*	Ranchhoddas Shamaldas Chanchad (Rancho)/ Phunsukh Wangdu	Kareena Kapoor, Boman Irani, R. Madhavan, Sharman Joshi, Omi Vaidya, Mona Singh
2008	*Ghajini*	Sanjay Singhania/Sachin	Asin, Pradeep Singh Rawat, Tinnu Anand, Jiah Khan
2007	*Taare Zameen Par*	Ram Shankar Nikumbh	Darsheel Safary, Tanay Chheda, Tisca Chopra, Vipin Sharma
2006	*Fanaa*	Rehan Quadri	Kajol, Tabu, Rishi Kapoor, Kirron Kher
2006	*Rang De Basanti*	Daljeet 'DJ'/ Chandrashekhar Azad	Siddharth, Sharman Joshi, Kunal Kapoor, Atul Kulkarni, R. Madhavan, Soha Ali Khan, Alice Patten
2005	*Mangal Pandey: The Rising*	Mangal Pandey	Rani Mukherjee, Toby Stephens, Coral Beed, Ameesha Patel, Varsha Usgaonkar, Kirron Kher, Mukesh Tiwari, Amin Hajee, Dibyendu Bhattacharya, Subrat Dutta, Ahsan Baksh, Irfanouzzaman
2001	*Dil Chahta Hai*	Akash Malhotra	Saif Ali Khan, Akshaye Khanna, Preity Zinta, Sonali Kulkarni, Dimple Kapadia

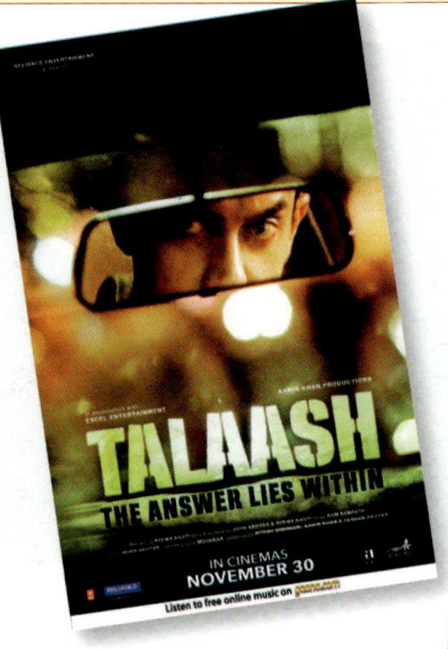

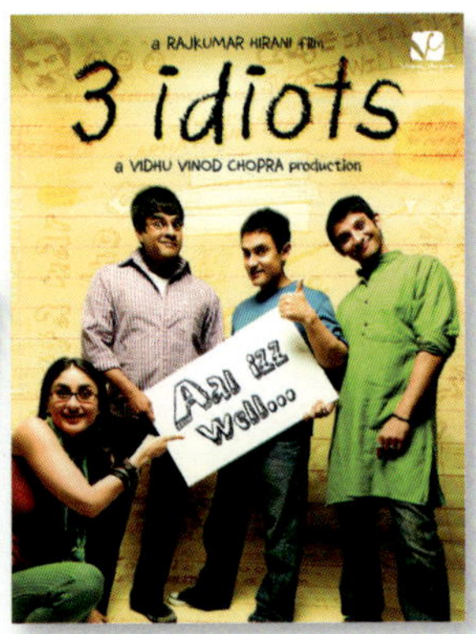

Director	Producer(s)	Story	Screenplay/Dialogue	Music
Vijay Krishna Acharya	Yash Raj Films	Vijay Krishna Acharya	Prakash Bharadwaj	Pritam
Reema Kagti	Ritesh Sidhwani, Farhan Akhtar, Aamir Khan	Reema Kagti, Zoya Akhtar	Farhan Akhtar, Anurag Kashyap (additional dialogue)	Ram Sampath
Kiran Rao	Aamir Khan, Kiran Rao	Kiran Rao	Kiran Rao	Gustavo Santaolalla
Rajkumar Hirani	Vidhu Vinod Chopra	Rajkumar Hirani, Abhijat Joshi	Vidhu Vinod Chopra (screenplay associate), Rajkumar Hirani, Abhijat Joshi	Shantanu Moitra
A.R. Murugadoss	Tagore Madhu, Madhu Mantena Varma	A.R. Murugadoss	A.R. Murugadoss; Piyush Mishra (dialogue)	A.R. Rahman
Aamir Khan	Aamir Khan	Amole Gupte	Amole Gupte	Shankar-Ehsaan-Loy
Kunal Kohli	Aditya Chopra, Yash Chopra	Shibani Bathija	Shibani Bathija	Jatin-Lalit
Rakeysh Omprakash Mehra	Rakeysh Omprakash Mehra, David Reid, Ronnie Screwvala	Kamlesh Pandey	Rakeysh Omprakash Mehra, Renzil D'Silva	A.R. Rahman
Ketan Mehta	Deepa Sahi and Bobby Bedi	Farrukh Dhondy	Farrukh Dhondy; Ranjit Kapoor (Hindi dialogue)	A.R. Rahman
Farhan Akhtar	Ritesh Sidwani, Farhan Akhtar, Pravin Talreja (co-producer)	Farhan Akhtar, Kassim Jagmagia (story co-developer)	Farhan Akhtar	Shankar-Ehsaan-Loy

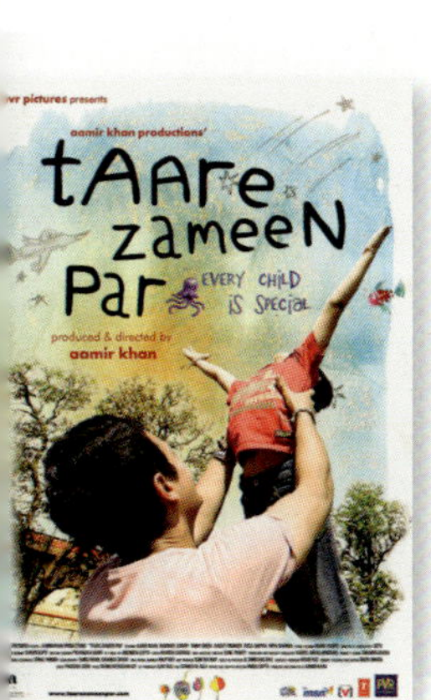

Year	Film	Role	Co-starring
2001	*Lagaan: Once Upon a Time in India*	Bhuvan	Gracy Singh, Rachel Shelley, Paul Blackthorne, Suhasini Mulay, Kulbhushan Kharbanda, Raghuveer Yadav, Rajendra Gupta, Rajesh Vivek, Shri Vallabh Vyas, Rajendranath Zutshi, Akhilendra Mishra, Pradeep Rawat, Daya Shankar Pandey, Yashpal Sharma, Amin Hajee, Aditya Lakhia, A.K. Hangal
2000	*Mela*	Kishan Pyare	Twinkle Khanna, Faisal Khan, Johnny Lever, Asrani, Tiku Talsania, Tinnu Verma
1999	*Earth* (*1947 Earth*)	Dil Navaz	Nandita Das, Kulbhushan Kharbanda, Kitu Gidwani, Raghuveer Yadav, Rahul Khanna, Arif Zakaria
1999	*Mann*	Dev Karan Singh	Manisha Koirala, Sharmila Tagore, Dipti Bhatnagar, Dalip Tahil, Anil Kapoor, Rani Mukherjee
1999	*Sarfarosh*	ACP Ajay Singh Rathod	Naseeruddin Shah, Sonali Bendre, Mukesh Rishi, Akash Khurana, Smita Jaykar
1998	*Ghulam*	Siddharth Marathe	Rani Mukherjee, Mita Vashisht, Rajit Kapoor, Sharat Saxena, Deepak Tijori, Dalip Tahil
1997	*Ishq*	Raja	Juhi Chawla, Kajol, Ajay Devgn
1996	*Raja Hindustani*	Raja Hindustani	Karisma Kapoor, Suresh Oberoi, Archana Puran Singh, Farida Jalal, Tiku Talsania, Mohnish Bahl, Kunal Khemu, Pramod Mouthu, Johnny Lever, Navneet Nishan, Veeru Krishnan

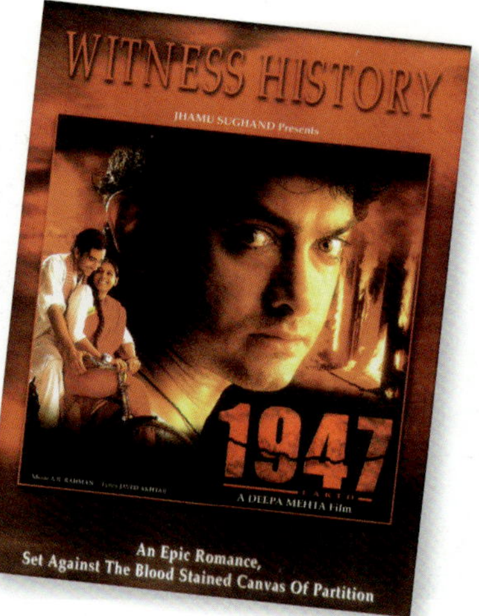

Director	Producer(s)	Story	Screenplay/Dialogue	Music
Ashutosh Gowariker	Aamir Khan	Ashutosh Gowariker	Ashutosh Gowariker, Kumar Dave and Sanjay Dayma (screenplay); K.P. Saxena (dialogue)	A.R. Rahman
Dharmesh Darshan	Umed Jain, Raksha Mistry	Dharmesh Darshan	Robin Bhatt, Sanjeev Duggal and Neeraj Vora (screenplay); Dharmesh Darshan and Neeraj Vora (dialogue)	Anu Malik, Surendra Sodhi
Deepa Mehta	Anne Masson, Deepa Mehta; David Hamilton and Jhamu Sughand (executive producers)	Bapsi Sidhwa	Deepa Mehta	A.R. Rahman
Indra Kumar	Ashok Thakeria, Indra Kumar	Noshir Khatow (story advisor)	Aatish Kapadia	Darshan Rathod, Sanjeev Rathod, Naresh Sharma
John Mathew Matthan	John Mathew Matthan	John Mathew Matthan	John Mathew Matthan (screenplay); Pathik Vats and Hriday Lani (dialogue)	Jatin-Lalit
Vikram Bhatt	Mukesh Bhatt	Anjum Rajabali	Anjum Rajabali	Jatin-Lalit
Indra Kumar	Gordhan Tanwani	Praful Parekh and Rajeev Kaul, Noshir Khatow (story advisor)	Praful Parekh and Rajeev Kaul (screenplay); Tanveer Khan (dialogue)	Anu Malik
Dharmesh Darshan	Aly Morani, Karim Morani, Bunty Soorma	Dharmesh Darshan	Dharmesh Darshan and Robin Bhatt (screenplay); Javed Siddiqui (dialogue)	Nadeem-Shravan

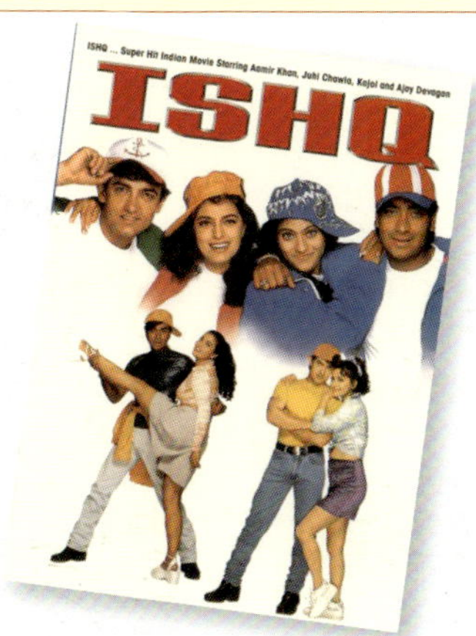

Year	Film	Role	Co-starring
1995	*Akele Hum Akele Tum*	Rohit Kumar	Manisha Koirala, Master Adil, Rohini Hattangadi, Paresh Rawal, Satish Shah, Deven Verma, Rakesh Roshan, Shafi Inamdar
1995	*Rangeela*	Munna	Jackie Shroff, Urmila Matondkar, Reema Lagoo, Gulshan Grover
1995	*Aatank Hi Aatank*	Rohan	Rajnikanth, Juhi Chawla, Archana Joglekar, Kabir Bedi, Om Puri, Pooja Bedi, Dalip Tahil, Raza Murad, Goga Kapoor
1995	*Baazi*	Inspector Amar Damjee	Mamta Kulkarni, Paresh Rawal, Avtar Gill, Kulbhushan Kharbanda, Raza Murad, Puneet Issar
1994	*Andaz Apna Apna*	Amar Manohar	Salman Khan, Raveena Tandon, Karisma Kapoor, Paresh Rawal, Mehmood, Tiku Talsania
1993	*Hum Hain Rahi Pyar Ke*	Rahul Malhotra	Juhi Chawla, Master Sharokh, Kunal Khemu, Baby Ashrafa
1993	*Parampara*	Ranbir Prithvi Singh	Sunil Dutt, Vinod Khanna, Anupam Kher, Saif Ali Khan, Raveena Tandon, Neelam Kothari, Ashwini Bhave, Ramya Krishnan
1992	*Isi Ka Naam Zindagi*	Chhotu	Farha Naaz, Asrani
1992	*Jo Jeeta Wohi Sikandar*	Sanjaylal Sharma	Ayesha Jhulka, Deepak Tijori, Kulbhushan Kharbanda, Pooja Bedi, Mamik
1992	*Daulat Ki Jung*	Rajesh Chaudhry	Juhi Chawla, Shafi Inamdar, Paresh Rawal, Kader Khan, Kiran Kumar, Dalip Tahil

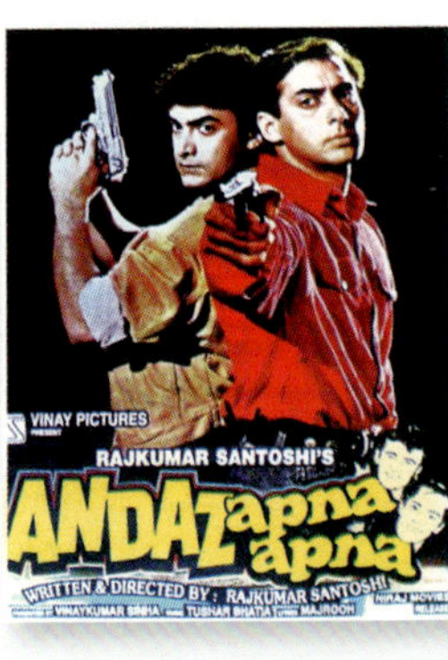

Director	Producer(s)	Story	Screenplay/Dialogue	Music
Mansoor Khan	Ratan Jain	Mansoor Khan	Nasir Hussain	Anu Malik
Ram Gopal Varma	Ram Gopal Varma	Ram Gopal Varma	Sanjay Chhel and Neeraj Vora (dialogue)	A.R. Rahman
Dilip Shankar	Mangal	Dilip Shankar	Iqbal Durrani (dialogue)	Bappi Lahiri, Samir Vibhaas
Ashutosh Gowariker	Salim Akhtar	Ashutosh Gowariker	Ashutosh Gowariker	Anu Malik
Rajkumar Santoshi	Vinay Kumar Sinha, Shanti Sinha (associate producer)	Rajkumar Santoshi	Rajkumar Santoshi (screenplay & dialogue); Dilip Shukla (dialogue)	Tushar Bhatia
Mahesh Bhatt	Tahir Hussain, Zeenat Hussain (co-producer) and Raj Khandelwal (executive producer)	Robin Bhatt, Sujit Sen	Robin Bhatt (also script); Aamir Khan (screenplay & script)	Nadeem-Shravan
Yash Chopra	Firoz A. Nadiawala	Honey Irani	Honey Irani and Aditya Chopra (screenplay); Rahi Masoom Reza and Surendra Prakash (dialogue)	Shiv-Hari
Kalidas	Ratan Mukherjee	Manoj Mitra	Ramesh Pant	Bappi Lahiri
Mansoor Khan	Nasir Hussain	Mansoor Khan	Mansoor Khan (screenplay); Nasir Hussain (dialogue)	Jatin-Lalit
S.A. Kader	Jalil Ahmed	Peeyush Sapru	Nawab Arzoo (screenplay); Akhtar Sohail (dialogue)	Anand-Milind

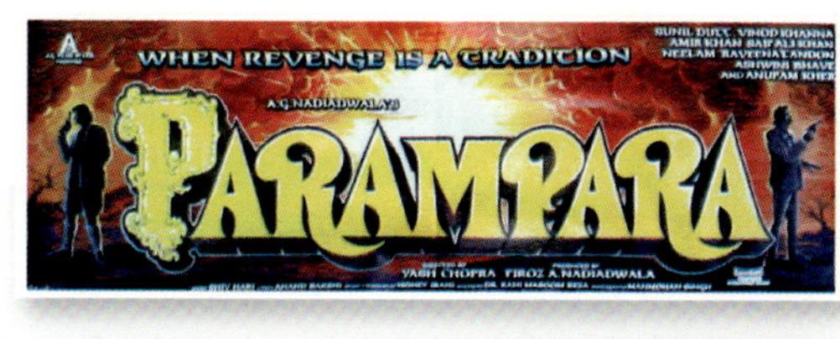

Year	Film	Role	Co-starring
1991	*Dil Hai Ke Manta Nahin*	Raghu Jetley	Pooja Bhatt, Anupam Kher, Tiku Talsania, Deepak Tijori
1991	*Afsana Pyar Ka*	Raj	Neelam, Deepak Tijori
1990	*Jawani Zindabad*	Shashi Sharma	Farha Naaz, Javed Jaffrey, Utpal Dutt, Asrani, Sushma Seth
1990	*Deewana Mujh Sa Nahin*	Ajay Sharma	Madhuri Dixit, Khushboo, Jainendra
1990	*Dil*	Raja Prasad	Madhuri Dixit, Saeed Jaffrey, Deven Verma, Anupam Kher, Johnny Lever
1990	*Tum Mere Ho*	Shiva	Juhi Chawla, Rajendranath Zutshi, Ajit Vachani, Sudhir Pandey
1990	*Awwal Number*	Sunny	Dev Anand, Ekta Sohini, Aditya Pancholi, Neeta Puri, Parikshat Sahni, Ram Mohan
1989	*Love Love Love*	Amit Verma	Juhi Chawla, Gulshan Grover, Dalip Tahil, Raza Murad, Om Shivpuri
1989	*Raakh*	Amir Hussein	Supriya Pathak, Pankaj Kapur, Naina Balsaver, Jagdeep
1988	*Qayamat Se Qayamat Tak*	Raj Singh	Juhi Chwala, Reema Lagoo, Dalip Tahil, Alok Nath, Rajendranath Zutshi, Goga Kapoor
1984	*Holi*	Madan Sharma	Naseeruddin Shah, Om Puri, Dr Shreeram Lagoo, Ashutosh Gowariker, Deepti Naval, Rahul Ranade
1973	*Yaadon Ki Baaraat*	Young Ratan (child artiste)	Dharmendra, Zeenat Aman, Vijay Arora, Ajit Khan, Tariq

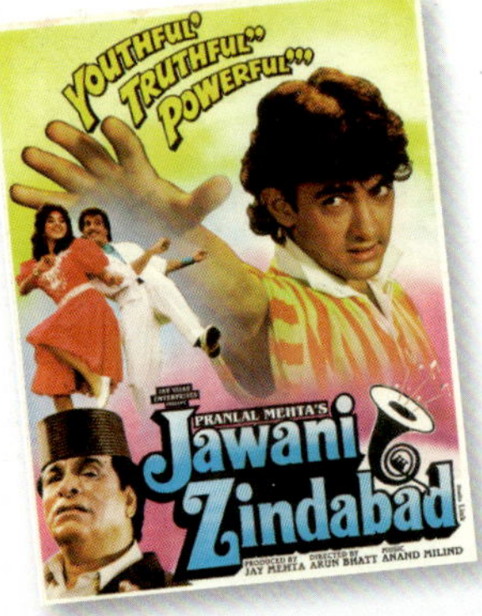

Director	Producer(s)	Story	Screenplay/Dialogue	Music
Mahesh Bhatt	Gulshan Kumar, Mukesh Bhatt (executive producer)	Robin Bhatt	Robin Bhatt (screenplay); Sharad Joshi (dialogue)	Nadeem-Shravan
M.R. Shahjahan	Sanjay Seksaria and Manoj Seksaria	Bono Deb	Bono Deb (screenplay); Ramesh Pant (dialogue)	Bappi Lahiri
Arun Bhatt	Jay Mehta	Bhushan Banmali	Bhushan Banmali (screenplay), Rahi Masoom Reza (dialogue)	Anand-Milind
Y. Nageshwar Rao	Ajit Parshotam, B.L. Ramchand (co-producer)	M. Parvez	M. Parvez	Anand-Milind
Indra Kumar	Indra Kumar, Ashok Thakeria	Praful Parekh, Rajiv Kaul and Noshir Khatow (story advisor)	Praful Parekh and Rajiv Kaul (screenplay); Kamlesh Pandey (dialogue)	Anand-Milind
Tahir Hussain	Tahir Hussain; Nikhat Khan, Faisal Khan and Zohra Begum (co-producers)	Tahir Hussain, Surendra Singh	Kalim Rahi (screenplay); Madan Joshi (dialogue)	Anand-Milind
Dev Anand	Dev Anand	Dev Anand	Dev Anand	Bappi Lahiri
Babbar Subhash	Babbar Subhash	Babbar Subhash	Babbar Subhash	Bappi Lahiri
Aditya Bhattacharya	Asif Noor	Aditya Bhattacharya	Aditya Bhattacharya (screenplay); Nuzhat Khan (dialogue)	Ranjit Barot
Mansoor Khan	Nasir Hussain	Nasir Hussain	Nasir Hussain	Anand-Milind
Ketan Mehta	Film Unit Productions	Mahesh Elkunchwar	Mahesh Elkunchwar and Ketan Mehta (screenplay); Hriday Lani (dialogue)	Rajat Dholakia
Nasir Hussain	Nasir Hussain	Salim-Javed	Salim-Javed (screenplay); Nasir Hussain (dialogue)	Rahul Dev Burman

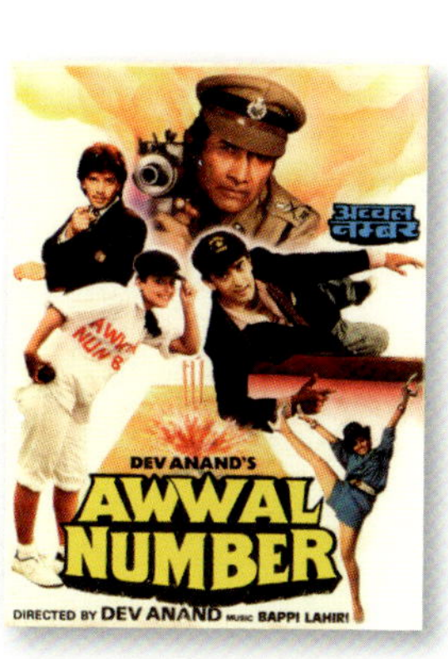

As updated on December 2013, excluding guest/special appearances and films that Aamir Khan produced, but did not act in like *Jaane Tu... Ya Jaane Na*, *Peepli (Live)* and so on.

ACKNOWLEDGEMENTS

The content and pictures used in this book are based on various sources, interviews and reference material that I could lay my hands upon. People from different fields of the film fraternity have been of great support to me.

I am grateful to Rajat Sharma for writing the Foreword and sharing small details about Aamir, the person. I wish to thank all the guest writers—Rauf Ahmed, Mayank Shekhar, Narendra Kusnur and Vikas Chandra Sinha—for their valuable contributions and inputs. Thanks to Raina for writing a beautiful poem on the actor.

I am obliged to Dr Mukesh Batra for all his support and Balakrishna Pillai (Spin Communique) for his valuable observations. I would also like to acknowledge Priyanka Chandra-Sinha and Juhi S for providing editorial help and assistance in writing the text.

I am indebted to the people who have helped me gain insights to Aamir, the actor—directors Indra Kumar and John Mathew Matthan, producer Ashok Thakeria, actor Gulshan Grover, publicity designers Aatmanand (Studio Link) and Rahul Nanda, columnist Ayaz Menon, painter J.P. Singhal, fashion designer Dinesh Singhal and painter Samir Mondal.

A big thank you to my photographer colleagues—Amol Kamble, Bidisha Roy, Durga Prasad, Hemant Rawat, Sachin Gokhale (Firstpost.com), Umesh Goswami, Spice PR, Dinodia Photo Agency, Mahindra & Mahindra, Napol Entertainment Pvt. Ltd. and *The Week* for contributing photographs along with film historian S.M.M. Ausaja for sharing pictures from his archives. My best regards to Ashok Dabhade, Ganesh Shinde and Mithun Singh for their visual inputs.

I really appreciate the efforts put in by artists Partho Chatterjee and Rajesh Srivastava for painting exclusive pictures of Aamir for this book.

I am extremely grateful to my publishers, Bikash and Tultul Niyogi for showing tremendous enthusiasm and patience while creating this book. Shaurya Shaukat Sircar deserves special mention for editing and shaping the book to what it is presently.

Last but not the least I owe a debt of gratitude to my wife Veena Chandra for enduring my obsession with Aamir Khan for an extended period.

SOURCES

Resources referred to in this book are:

Pali Hill: The Beverly Hills of Mumbai

Open magazine
The Times of India (interviews)
The Economic Times
The Indian Express
Hindustan Times, 18 Nov. 2012, Afsana Ahmad
HT Café
TIME magazine
India Today, Jan. 2010
CineBlitz

www.masala.com
www.daijiworld.com
www.bollyguide.com
www.newsbullet.in

***QSQT*: Launching of the Boy Next Door**

The Illustrated Weekly of India
Zee Premier
Filmfare
The Week
CineBlitz
Tehelka
Fress Press Journal, Glam Wednesday, 28 Dec. 2011
India Today, Jan. 2010

***Lagaan*: Pangs of a First-Time Producer**

The Spirit of Lagaan by Satyajit Bhatkal
TIME magazine
India Today, Jan. 2010
Tehelka magazine, 17 Apr. 2012
The Illustrated Weekly of India, 19-20 Jan. 1991
Filmfare, December issue

Take Two: Turning to Meaningful Cinema and Direction

Tehelka magazine
HT Café
Filmfare
CineBlitz
Bombay Times

At Home: The Family Man

CineBlitz, May 2011
The Week
Mumbai Mirror
Screen
India Today, Jan. 2010

***Satyamev Jayate*: A Love Letter to India**

TIME magazine
The Free Press Journal
The Hindu
Hindustan Times

INDEX